LETTERS FROM JESUS

BY ALLAN DESCHENEAU

CONTENTS

ACKNOWLEDGEMENTS & DEDICATION

I am so very thankful for the people who contributed to this book. It is my first, and I'm not certain how many will follow, but these people have made it a wonderful experience.

I want to begin by noting that I am particularly indebted to great authors like Dr. David Jeremiah, Warren Wiersbe, Rick Warren, Bill Hybels, and so many others who, through their books and sermons, have shared with me such wisdom. I am especially thankful to Mark Driscoll who, though I have never met, has had a remarkable impact on my life and ministry. This book would not exist without these great men of God.

Also, I am so very grateful to Sue Meehan and Sam Malone for taking the time out of their life to fix the many, many, *many* grammatical errors that pervaded the manuscript! What would I do without you both? Thanks also to Pierre Belanger for designing the beautiful cover of this book in his free time… which he has very little of.

Thank you also to those in my church family at Nepean Baptist Church, and those who came before (you know who you are!) who have shown such love and helped me so much. You were the testing ground for this material, and you were very patient, kind and encouraging as I presented it.

I want to dedicate this first book to my family. Especially to my *amazing* wife Anita, who proves daily just how remarkable she really is. I can't imagine my life or ministry without you! To my kids Ethan, Edison and Erica who have taught me far more about God than anyone I have ever met (or probably will *ever meet*). And of course, to my brand new, beautiful baby Eowyn! I look forward to getting to know you.

Finally, and most importantly, I want to give my dedication, acknowledgment, worship and thanks to my Lord and Saviour Jesus Christ. It is He who has given me the passion and ability to write, to teach, and to preach His amazing Word. All glory to Him in the highest and Him alone!

HOW TO USE THIS BOOK

Before you dive headlong into this book, I want to take a moment of your time to help you get the most out of it that you can.

The content of this book was originally presented as a series of sermons, and I've since added, edited and generally cleaned it up as much as I could to present it to you. My prayer for the sermon series, and for this book, is that God would be able to use the words within for His glory, to challenge, help, correct, train, deepen and sharpen His people in worship, service and love.

For Individuals

If you have come across this book and are a Christian, then let me encourage you to read this book as a journey. Walk along with the letter carrier of the Roman Road and experience the cities he visits for the first time. Spend time in each chapter and city getting to know the history, the culture, and the church. Then commit yourself to learning whatever lesson God has for you there before strapping on your sandals again and setting off for your next locale.

Some of the cities and churches may make a deeper impact than others, while some may leave you with hardly any impression at all. That's ok! Just listen and learn as much as you can, and enjoy the trip. When you feel God stopping your little tour and saying, "Hold up, this is for you," pause, pray and perhaps journal in the margin what you hear God saying to you.

Later, at the end of the book I have written a "Reflective Exercise" called "Jesus' Letter to Me" in which you will, effectively, go back over your journey, develop the photos you've taken, ponder the high-lights, and consider more closely what Jesus wants to say to you. The pencil marks and margin notes you've been making along the way may help you look back more effectively.

There are also some "Suggested Devotional Readings and Questions." If you want to get the most out of this study, begin each chapter by reading the passage (which I encourage for everyone), and then end each chapter by answering the question. Ponder that question in your heart for a time, until you read the next chapter.

For Groups

If you are going through this book as a small group, study group, home group, or even synchronized swimming group (be careful not to get the book wet!), let me encourage you to read a chapter per week, high-lighter and pencil in hand. Mark the sentences or concepts that impact you, that you feel God wants you to mull over, or that you have questions about, and bring them to the discussion group to share.

After each study assign the "Suggested Devotional Readings and Question" of the week to each member to answer *in writing*. When you get together again, begin your discussions with prayer, and then by talking about how you answered the question of the week.

For Ministers

If you are a pastor, minister or lay-leader in a church, then GOD BLESS YOU! I appreciate you all, and would love to share a large Tim Horton's coffee with three milks with you some time (Ok, maybe not *share...* you can have your own).

As I said, most of the content in this book was originally presented as a sermon series to my church. I did a lot of research and pray that the information given here is of the best quality and accuracy. If not, please forgive me... (Hey, you're a Christian, you have to.)

Feel free to preach or teach this series! It was written to glorify God and build up His people, and if it can help you do so in your context, please do so. Go ahead and use the illustrations and content, but *please* make sure that your congregation or class knows that you are borrowing them from another source. (If you need a wake up call in this regard, re-read Jeremiah 23:30.)

Finally, if you need any help, then please feel free to contact me anytime. I have already done all of the PowerPoint presentations, and would be happy to pass them along if you want them. You can find my contact info on my blog at www.ArtoftheChristianNinja.com.

Suggested Devotional Readings & Questions

Reading 1: Revelation 1:1-20
"Introduction: Jesus in the Midst"
Reflection Question: Contrast John's portrait of Jesus in verses 12-18 with Isaiah's in Isaiah 53. What does this tell you about Jesus?

Reading 2: Revelation 2:1-7
"Ephesus: Love in Priority"
Reflection Question: When you reflect on what you have done this week, what do your thoughts and actions say about your "first love?"

Reading 3: Revelation 2:8-11
"Smyrna: Facing Persecution"
Reflection Question: What benefits have you (or others you know) had from facing suffering and persecution?

Reading 4: Revelation 2:12-17
"Pergamum: Flank Attacks"
Reflection Question: Do you have any secret sins in your life where the flank attacks of the enemy are compromising your walk with Jesus?

Reading 5: Revelation 2:18-28
"Thyatira: Compromised Morality"
Reflection Question: How do you feel about the word "sin?" Is it too harsh? Does it make you uncomfortable? Should it be used more or less often?

Reading 6: Revelation 3:1-6
"Sardis: Reputation and Reality"
Reflection Question: Are you truly spiritually alive, or do you merely "have a reputation of being alive?" When was the last time you connected with Jesus?

Reading 7: Revelation 3:7-13
"Philadelphia: The Open Door"
Reflection Question: Is Jesus opening a door for you because you are faithful, or do you find yourself banging up against closed doors and wondering why you aren't progressing in your spiritual walk?

Reading 8: Revelation 3:14-22
"Laodicea: Sophisticated or Sanctified"
Reflection Question: How deep is your "need" for God today, or do you "not need a thing?"

MAP OF THE CITIES IN REVELATION
MAP COURTESY OF MIKE CAMPBELL

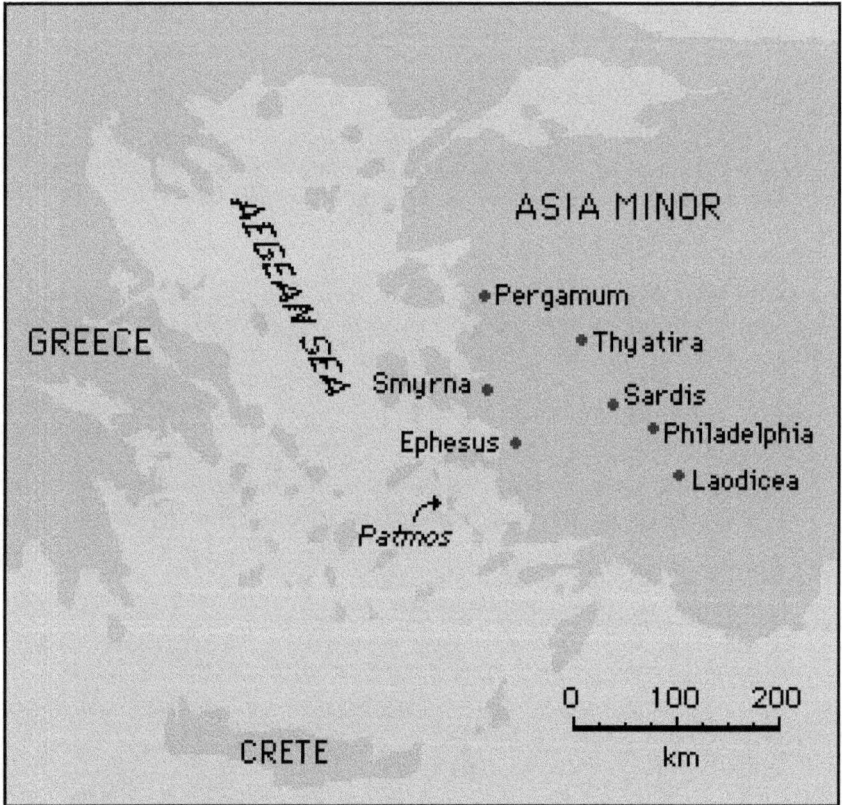

CHAPTER ONE

Introduction: Ten Speeds and Thin Ice

Beware - thin ice

There are many things in this world that rock our boats and shake us up. I remember many different times in my youth, as I'm sure you can as well, where I found myself coasting along, comfortable, relaxed and … "normal." Times when all was well … and then in a split second, in mere moments, everything seemed to snap out of joint and life changed forever.

There are times that stick in your mind as moguls, or touch points that you look back to as stirring, jolting, emotional, fearsome, or character building. Some people look back at these times and say things like, "it was that moment when I found out who I was, or what I was capable of." "It was a time like that when everything stopped … everything changed … everything seemed different after that."

I'll give you a small example from my own life. I remember riding my bike down the hill in my home town of Hinton, Alberta. In Hinton, which was built on the foothills of the Rocky Mountains, you were almost always either going uphill or down. Case in point, it took me 5 minutes to bike from my house to the high school in the morning … it took me 45 minutes to bike back home in the afternoon.

I remember a time when I was riding my bike down the hill, moving faster and faster, racing my friends to the bottom. Uncharacteristically, I was actually out in front during this race, and I was really picking up speed. I was flying down the hill, going below the highway overpasses above, passing cars to the left of me. My 10 speed was going as fast as it was capable of …I'm sure the designers of this bike didn't think it would be able to move as fast as I had it going that day.

Then, in the briefest of seconds, I looked down to see where my tires were. I had heard a strange noise … a noise that 10 speed bicycles are not supposed to make … a grinding sound that was coming from below. I looked down to see my front tire stuck in a rut in the cement. It was only about the width of my tire, but it was deep enough that I knew it was going to take some kind of skill to get out. Sadly, I'm not built with that kind of skill. I couldn't turn. I couldn't lean. I could only go straight in the direction that the groove was leading me … and it was leading me into the enormous cement support of the next overpass.

Have you ever heard the saying, "sometimes you're the bug, sometimes you're the windshield?" If I didn't get out of that rut, I was going to be the bug. All of this processing was happening in seconds. I quickly considered my options. The option I felt best suited the situation was this: I would pull up as hard as I could on the handle bars, and try to hop out of the rut. It seemed sensible at the time. So I did it. With as much grace and force as I could muster I grabbed the handle bars and popped the front tire out of the groove. For about an eighth of a second, I thought I was fine … until I realized the fatal flaw in my plan … my bike had two wheels. The back wheel was still stuck, but now it was moving in a different direction than the front wheel. For those who are familiar with the intricacies of high-speed biking, you will understand the importance of both wheels moving in the same direction. And you can imagine what happened next.

One wheel went one way, one wheel went another. Terror gripped my 10-year-old brain and I smashed into the pavement, skidding along for what felt like about a block or two. Pain, scars, misery, dirt, blood and sweat. A sudden moment that brought quick changes and desperate acts into my short little life. What began as a simple bike ride turned into a memory that will forever be burned into my mind.

Do you have any of those? I'm sure you do. Times that seemed innocuous at first, but in split seconds seemed to blossom into something remarkable. Of course, it doesn't have to be something bad or traumatic. It can be a good memory too. The moment you find out you or your wife is pregnant, winning your first race, a birthday surprise, or the first bite of that AAA Alberta, perfectly marinated, barbequed steak. Life changing times.

Unfortunately, what tends to stick in our minds are the more traumatic, more frightening moments. For whatever reason, they seem to fuse most effectively into the synapses of our brains. This is probably why we are reminded to count our blessings and remember God's faithfulness so many times in the Bible. Let me give you another example of one of these tough times.

My parents built a new log cabin home a couple years ago. I've been there only once, but it was really nice. They finally got out of town, and moved into a tiny little piece of heaven about 35 minutes from where I grew up. It's a great new place where you can hike, ride motor bikes or quads, have a nice fire, and just get away. There's a lake within walking distance that is the perfect size to take a little canoe and paddle around. They even keep it stocked with fish. In the winter time it freezes over, and though some people like to ice fish and skate on it, it's not recommended.

On the far end of the lake is a set of agitators. They stir up the water, aerate it, and keep it healthy for the fish. They are sort of like the bubble machines in an aquarium, but much bigger. In the winter, as the rest of the lake freezes, the areas around those agitators don't ... or if they do, it's very thin ice.

Warnings are posted on every road in, and on every path that leads to the lake. "Stay away from the agitators," "Don't walk on the ice," "For your own safety, stay off the lake in the winter." Back home, and I'm sure it's the same everywhere, there's a saying, "There's no such thing as safe ice." One phrase that's on every one of the signs is this: "At own risk." In other words ... "You have been warned."

Some do skate though. Some ice fish, others like to bring their snow-mobiles, quads, and even cars onto the ice. And every year, someone ... actually a few someones ... end up having one of those "moments" that I talked about before. My brother likes to keep me informed about them. "Guess who went into the lake this year?" has come up in a few of our conversations. They say if you go to the bottom of Miller's Lake, that you can have your pick of snow-mobiles and ice fishing equipment. Every year people fall through. It's almost an annual tradition.

Despite the warning signs, despite everyone knowing the stories, people get themselves into the same precarious situation every year. Not one dissimilar to the one I had on my bike as a kid. Their life, moving along just fine, everything ahead of them … maybe it even looks like they are winning the race … and then seemingly stuck moving in a direction towards a place that they don't want to go. One second they are having fun, and the next they are feeling the biting cold as they struggle for the edge of the ice in Miller's Lake. I don't think anyone has ever lost their life to that lake yet, but many have lost their gear, and their confidence, despite the signs and stories of warning.

Sometimes I wonder if the Christian church and some individuals make the same mistake. There have been, and still are, copious amounts of signs and stories surrounding the church, giving encouragement, direction, and warnings to humanity as to the things they need to do and avoid to stay healthy and live a happy and profitable life. There are guidelines to follow, and many stories of how people have gotten themselves into trouble. And yet, we continue to venture out onto the thin ice, and many individuals, Christian or not, even whole groups of people and churches … have fallen through the cracks … and sadly, many have been lost.

This is the thought and prayer that is going to drive our study through the beginning of the book of Revelation. One of the things that I hope will be pounded home during the next eight weeks is that these next couple of chapters are the literal and authoritative words of Jesus Christ. God Himself is talking here. They are His special instructions, exhortations, warnings and commands to a series of churches, recorded for us to read and learn from. Jesus, in His divine wisdom and mercy, gave these words to John to not only pass along to these seven historical churches, but also to record and preserve them for us today.

Jesus not only writes these letters to churches and groups of people or pastors who are treading out and fall through the thin ice … but to individuals as well. God gave us His word to teach, correct, rebuke and train us for life, and there are many who are not listening to it, outside and inside the church. And so they are treading on thin ice. Whether they acknowledge it or not, they are walking on dangerous paths, on uncertain ground.

Each decision, another point of pressure on the ice, each step another potential fracture beneath them. Sometimes they hear the cracks, they begin to sense and feel the danger, and they acknowledge their limitations, heed the posted signs and choose to get back to the safety of firm ground. But more often than not, they press forward despite the warnings in their hearts and all around them, despite the cracks beneath their feet, and despite that voice inside of them that says they should listen to the signs and turn back. Sometimes it takes a dangerous plunge through broken ice into frigid and painful waters for some people to wake up to the danger of their path. Sadly for some, that first plunge is their last.

Consider some people's reaction to the rampage at Dawson College in Montreal that happened September 2006 where one woman was killed and 19 were wounded, or the shootings at Virginia Tech in April 2007, and the loss of those 34 lives. They were true and terrible catastrophes. I in no way want to belittle or misinterpret the pain of those who are grieving. I simply want to use them to make a point. Consider the many mixed reactions, and the various perspectives that we have seen on the situation, on the news, in the papers, and through other media. I don't mean the victims, or the shooters ... but those around them.

Some, whose lives were already on thin ice (and many college students are treading farther and farther out there during their years in post-secondary), saw this as a sign to re-evaluate their position and turn back. They began to ask questions about what their lives are built on, where their faith is, what their focus is on. They began to evaluate their choices, their family lives and their support systems. They looked at the situation, assessed where they were, and chose to find firmer ground to walk on.

For others who were on the thin ice, this plunged them below. Their faith in God, in humanity, in their religion, in themselves ... was shaken to the core and they lost their grounding. They found themselves floundering, surrounded by pain, weighed down by life, and with nothing to stand on to help them find security. This was a pain that they were not ready for, a loss that *wasn't meant for them*, something *they didn't deserve*, and something they had no mechanism to handle it with.

My prayer for these folks is that God would send someone out to them ... someone who has been on the ice and knows the way back to shore. Someone who can pull them out, and lead them to safety before the pain is too overwhelming and they succumb to it, and go under.

Some who experienced the tragedy were already on firm ground. You probably know the story of Dale Lang, the man who lost his son Jason on April 28th, 1999 in a copycat Columbine-style high school shooting in Taber, Alberta. His story of forgiveness and love has taught and helped many people come back from the brink during trying times. He, and people like him, see the same situation, experience the same trauma, and even lose loved ones. But they had made the choice some time before to walk away from the fracturing and unsteady ground their lives were built on, and stand on the firm ground.

These people had a support system already in place when this occurred … their small group or their church. They had an understanding about this world that others didn't … that parts of this existence are flawed and evil and these things will unfortunately happen. And these people have the ability to endure during these times because they have hope in the future. They can look at this tragedy and see the hands of God moving in it … or at least trust that they will eventually. The event didn't sink them, but gave them the chance to call out to others who were walking on the thin ice, and guide them back to the firm and solid ground they were on with Jesus.

That is effectively what Jesus is doing here throughout the next two chapters that we are going to study. In these seven letters to the churches, He is calling out to them … warning some that they are either way out on thin ice, or are heading there, and He is trying to guide them back to firm ground. He is looking into the hearts and lives of individuals and saying, "I see you moving towards danger, and I care about you too much to see you plunge into the icy water. Please, come back to me."

Throughout this study, I hope that each one of us can hear Jesus calling out to us. For some, He asks them to get their priorities straight. Others learn how to face persecution for their beliefs. Jesus addresses the importance of having firm doctrine, watching out for flank attacks, and acknowledging the critical role of moral purity. He challenges others to wake up and start living their lives. He challenges some to overcome the complacency that has overtaken their lives, and shake off the cobwebs that have built up.

I just want to give you a quick note on what we *won't* be studying. Revelation is an amazing book. It is full of prophecies, worship songs, rich imagery, poetry, angels, heavenly battles and descriptions of the future. Through the next eight chapters we are only going to scratch the surface of the book of Revelation. In fact, if this book was laid out by a modern publisher, I would say that we were not going to get much past the cover of the book, the dust jacket, the dedication and the introduction. I'm afraid that this book will have no bowls, no seals, no four horsemen, no Armageddon. Our purpose will be to examine what Jesus begins His letter with… the seven letters to the churches.

Each of us struggles in different areas, and some of us struggle with a few of them. My prayer is that as we begin to take the next steps into the future, that this series will convict and challenge us as a Church, and as individuals to thank God for our strengths, acknowledge our weaknesses, read the warning signs, see the cracks beneath our feet, and choose to turn back … or turn around for the first time … and head back to the solid ground of Biblical Christianity based on a right relationship with the Lord Jesus Christ.

CHAPTER TWO

The Revelation: Jesus in the Midst

Now, to begin our foray into these letters from Jesus, I just want to pull a few things out of the introductory chapter to get our minds started down this road. So, please, grab your Bible and go read Revelation Chapter 1. I'll wait here.

Done? Ok. John's prologue here, which if we use my former illustration of this being a modern publisher's book, we can see as the little bit of writing on the inside of the dust jacket. It seems designed to whet the reader's appetite. Today, if you want to get a quick glimpse of what a book is about, and get a flavour for the kind of story that is coming, you open the book up and take a look at the inside of the jacket. That's the kind of thing that I see John opening his book with here.

He says that what follows is about, "The revelation of Jesus Christ, which God gave him to show his servants what must soon take place. He made it known by sending his angel to his servant John, who testifies to everything he saw—that is, the word of God and the testimony of Jesus Christ. Blessed is the one who reads the words of this prophecy, and blessed are those who hear it and take to heart what is written in it, because the time is near" (1:1).

John gives us just a taste, *a hint* of what is to come in the rest of the book. John says in verse one that this is "the revelation of Jesus Christ." From the very first words, John gets the reader excited. Some people in history have called this book, "the Revelation of John," or "the Apocalypse of St John the Apostle." It's not. The words "revelation" and "apocalypse" don't really mean what most of us think of when we hear them. John says that this book is going to be the "revelation," the revealing, of Jesus.   New information, a new mystery explained; a revelation. That's what *apocalypse* really means … it has come to mean some kind of universal, widespread disaster … but that's not its origin. It was first used to describe a prophetic revelation. That's how it's used here … a new, prophetic revelation, all about Jesus Christ.

John says that this book is all about Jesus. It's not "the revelation of John." It's not something he made up. It's the revelation of Jesus … *to John*. That's what makes verse 3 more understandable. "When this book is read in public, or in private, it brings blessing to those who read it, and those who hear it … and take it to heart." When we take this revelation, this new understanding of Jesus, "to heart" and we carry it around with us each day, it brings us blessing.

Now take a look at the next part, starting in verse 4, that the NIV calls the "Greetings and Doxology." I see these more like the "Acknowledgements and Dedication" at the very beginning of the book. In almost every book I've read, there's a dedication. To the parents, to the wife, to the kids, to some teacher … this book is written and dedicated to so-and-so. Now, since Revelation is not really a book but a letter written to a group of churches, this isn't so much the dedication as it is the address and the greeting. Still with me? It tells us who the letter is for. But the great part of this section is that it goes way beyond the regular addressing of the letter… and it turns into a dedication and worship poem of sorts.

It's not just a letter "to the seven churches in the province of Asia"; it's a letter dedicated to the glory of God, to the work of the Holy Spirit, and to the worship of Jesus. This is why I see it as the dedication. John is dedicating this letter to God. Right off the bat John wants to make sure that the readers know that this is a book of worship. It's a book by Jesus, about Jesus, written for the glory of Jesus, to the churches of Jesus. Look at verse 5 and we get a sense of John's heart here. Jesus is the faithful, trustworthy "witness" whom we can count on to tell us the truth about God's Kingdom. He is the one we look to as "the firstborn of the dead," and the one who gives us the hope that we will be raised from death one day as well. He is the "king" to whom we devote our allegiance. John says that Jesus "loves us," "freed us," and took the role of the ancient priest, the only one who could approach the Holy of Holies where God lived ... and He made it available to everyone. His work on the cross "made us a kingdom of priests" that has full-time access to God, and has the blessing of serving Him with every part of our lives.

John goes on in his dedication to talk about the time that we will see Jesus again. It is sort of like when authors say, "This is why I'm dedicating my book to this person." Look at verse 7.

John says, one day, just like a mighty warrior stirs up clouds of dust behind his chariot as he rides to war, Jesus too is coming again, stirring up the clouds of heaven as He comes to wage the final war and bring judgment once and for all to those who persecute His people and refuse to bring allegiance to Him. This is not the meagre, marginalized, poor, first-century Galilean carpenter. This is the Lord and Master of the Universe. Jesus is revealed as the Alpha and the Omega, the God of the Old Testament and the New, the One who is with us today, who was orchestrating the past since time began, and who holds the future in His hands. John is saying, "THIS is who the book is about, and is dedicated to!" And that's just the first page!

Now I wish I had more time to take apart the next section; the one the NIV calls, "One like a Son of Man." This, if we use my modern book illustration, could be considered the writing on the back cover, or even the first couple of pages of the story. It sets the context of what is going to happen for the rest of the story. It describes the circumstances of the main characters. It gives part of the history of the author and introduces the kind of language and thought pattern that will spread through the rest of the book. It's all here in this little section.

For now, there is just a little bit that I want to draw out before we end this chapter. Jesus here is described in beautiful detail as John pulls in rich images and historical, Messianic language from all over the Bible. But I want to focus on one little part: Where Jesus is standing.

Read from verse 12. John says, "I turned around to see the voice that was speaking to me. And when I turned I saw seven golden lamp stands, and among the lamp stands was someone 'like a son of man'." Look down to verse 20 and we see a more complete picture. It says, "and the seven lamp stands are the seven churches."

Jesus is pictured here standing *among* His churches. That's the final picture I want to leave with you as we consider the journey we are about to take. Remember Jesus' promise in Matthew 18:20, "For where two or three come together in my name, there am I with them." He gave the same promise at the end in Matthew 28:20, "And surely I am with you always, to the very end of the age." This picture in Revelation of Jesus among the lamp stands is Jesus fulfilling those promises.

When we gather together, when we come together in our homes, in our churches, or anywhere to pray to and worship God … Jesus is there. Another translation of this passage in Revelation says that Jesus is "*in the midst*" of the seven lamp stands. The Greek word here is MESOS. It means that Jesus is "in the middle, in the centre of." In some contexts it's used to mean "filling the spaces in between" those who gather in His name. That's where Jesus is. He's not hovering above. Our prayers do not go through the ceiling. God isn't in the sky. He's near. He's "in the midst" of us. He's here.

Where we are … Jesus is. He's omnipresent. He can hear us, experience with us, and wants to be there for us. When Jesus writes these letters to these churches, and to us, He's not writing from afar … He's writing "in the midst." He's writing from the centre of them. He's with them, filling in the spaces, guiding, and calling them back from the thin ice they find themselves on.

My hope and prayer is that we can understand that. That in our lives, on the shifting ground we may find ourselves on sometimes … looking into the future of our lives, our families, our churches, our cities, and our nations, as we embark on this new adventure God is placing before us, that we can understand that Jesus is "in our midst," ready to save, serve, teach, redeem, and listen. Prepared to forgive our past wrongs, extend the hand of mercy and healing, to bring us back into relationship with Him, and to move us forward into effective ministry and vibrant, purposeful lives.

CHAPTER THREE

Ephesus: Love in Priority

Chapter one begins with a description of what John is seeing and hearing during his vision. He finds himself "in the Spirit" (vs. 10). The term "in the spirit" has a lot behind it. David Jeremiah teaches that it could mean, "*spiritized,*" meaning he is no longer where he was but has been sucked into some kind of alternate, spiritual dimension. It could mean that he was having a vision during his sleep. It could mean that he was in the same spot as usual, and Jesus came to Him and transformed the world around him. It could mean a lot of things. What is important is that we realize that he was in an alternate *reality.* Not something made up, or induced by a drug. Where he is during this revelation is no less real than where you or I am right now.

He finds himself "in the Spirit" and then he hears a voice telling him to, "Write on a scroll what you see and send it to the seven churches" (vs. 11). The voice is as loud as a trumpet and when he turns around to see who is speaking. He is struck by a vision of a man walking among seven lamp stands ... it was Jesus Christ as John had never seen Him before.

John had lived with Christ on earth for a few years, he had been at the cross when Jesus died, and had been the one that Jesus asked to take care of His mother Mary. John was there at the empty tomb, and he was also there when Jesus came into the room to show that He had conquered death and had risen to life. John had eaten with the risen Lord, and had been taught by Him. John was there on the Mount of Olives when Jesus ascended up into Heaven. But this person standing before him now was completely different. The man he knew as Jesus Christ was there ... but this was the glorified Christ, the One who shone with the glory of God! As a reaction to seeing Jesus in His glory, John tells us the story of what he is seeing. The one who had lived with Jesus for years, and was called "the one whom Jesus loved," possibly Jesus' best friend during His earthly ministry, "fell at his feet as though dead" (vs. 17), totally overcome by his vision of the glorified Lord.

In an amazing display of grace, mercy, and love, Jesus extends His hand and picks John up and says, "Do not be afraid." And then in verse 19 Jesus tells John what he will be doing for the next while. Jesus says, "Write, therefore, what you have seen, what is now and what will take place later." Jesus in essence says, "I'm going to show you some things and tell you some things. I'm going to give you a guided tour of the future, and I want you to write it down and then pass it along to these churches. I've also got some letters to send out, and I want you to take them down too." And Jesus begins by dictating a series of seven letters to John, each one to a specific church.

So John obeys immediately. We almost get the sense here that he whips out his pen, opens up his notebook, pulls up his chair to the table, and is ready to go. And Jesus begins his dictation to the first church, Ephesus.

Now, before we begin, I just have a few introductory notes on the letters in general.

First, and I want this to be at the forefront: Chapters 2 and 3 of Revelation are the recordings of seven *actual* letters from Jesus to seven *actual* churches in Asia Minor. They are real historical cities, not merely metaphors or made-up places. Ephesus, Smyrna, and Laodicea, are all first-century Roman cities. Some of these cities can still be visited today. These letters have also been preserved for us to read and learn from. In fact, these letters were not sent individually to the churches, but were all distributed together, so each church could read the other church's letters.

I believe, based on what the Bible says, this is because Jesus wants Christians to know each other's problems so we can hold each other accountable, share our troubles, pray for one another, judge each other, and hold each other up.

In every church today there are going to be different things to learn from each of the letters. Many churches will have individuals that make the mistakes of at least one or more of the seven churches, and many will have individuals who should be commended in the same way that Jesus commends them. So they are not only written to historical churches, but are also written to be authoritative and helpful for us to read today. And my prayer for the study will be that we will hear what Jesus is saying to these churches, mine out what it meant to them, and learn from it in terms of what He is saying to us as a Church and as individuals.

Second, these letters are from Jesus Christ. They are not from John the Apostle. Some commentaries write as though these are the words of John. As though he one day decided to write a bunch of letters to these churches, and then sign the name of Jesus to them. He didn't. These letters really are the words of Jesus specifically to these churches and to us. John is merely the scribe, writing down what Jesus wants to say. And as such, these letters are somewhat unique in their form. They do not conform to the way that people at that time wrote letters. In fact, they are a lot more like the ancient prophecies and declarations to Israel that were delivered by Old Testament prophets like Elijah -- the ones that usually had a "Thus sayeth the Lord" somewhere in them. The prophet would stand before the king or the people and would say, "I'm about to tell you what God told me to tell you ... Thus sayeth the Lord. I'm not making this up myself, God told me to tell you this. And you better listen. Thus sayeth the Lord." That's how these letters in Revelation read; they are forceful. They are not so much letters, as they are Royal Decrees from the presiding King to His people.

We aren't usually too fond of this concept. We'd much rather assume the Bible is full of niceties and pearls of wisdom that we can sew on pillows and hang on the walls of our offices. We'd much rather read all of the wonderful promises in the Bible, and maybe just get some of the soft-sell on some things that we have to change. We'd rather have a Jesus that says, "You may want to think about working on this, when you have the time, if you don't mind, maybe, please…"

There are a lot of words in these letters that are going to be tough to hear, especially in this nicey-nice, politically correct era of ours. For example, we're going to read the word "REPENT" a bunch of times

(Eeek! I don't like that word!). And it's going to happen over and over because this is what the King is saying MUST be done in His Kingdom.

Third, each letter has similarities in structure. Jesus seemed to write these letters in a certain way. They have repeating phrases and sections that contain important, yet personalized information for each church. For this study we will be looking at eight different elements in each letter. They are listed in each chapter so that you can easily follow along. So if you are not there already, go get your Bible again and open it up and read Revelation 2:1-7. Got it? No? REPENT!!! Ok, good.

The Address
Done? Ok. The first of the eight elements is always the address, "To the angel of the church in Ephesus write."

Let me give you a bit of a history of Ephesus. Ephesus was the closest city to the Isle of Patmos, where John was located (go ahead and look at the map at the beginning of the book), and would be the first stop for the letter carrier to make as he followed the Roman Road to take the letter on its journey. Ephesus was the 4th largest city in the Roman Empire, and was probably the most famous city in Asia Minor. It was not a capital city, but it was a great political centre, as well as a centre for commerce, art, music and tourism. Ephesus was situated about 3 miles away from the Aegean Sea, and it boasted a great harbour that opened up to the Caster River which allowed Ephesus to grow into one of the greatest trade cities of its day.

It was a beautiful city with great temples, including the Temple of Artemis, one of the Seven Wonders of the ancient world. It had an amphitheatre that could hold up to 25,000 people, where there would be great dramatic plays, artists, and political speakers.

Acts chapter 19 tells the story of the first Christian church planted in Ephesus by Paul and his friends Aquila and Priscilla. Timothy pastored the church of Ephesus for a time, and when Paul wrote to him in I and II Timothy, they were addressed this church.

According to Acts 19:10, the church of Ephesus became a very important evangelistic centre for about three years, enjoying a great and long-lasting time of ministry in the city itself and in the region beyond. They sent out many missionaries and had some great and powerful preachers. All the churches we see in this area were probably church plants that came from the seminary / church planting school that Paul set up in Ephesus. The Apostle John was closely associated with the church in Ephesus, and probably preached and attended there in his later years.

It is thought that he even wrote his Gospel from Ephesus. In fact, after John was released from exile, he went back to minister in Ephesus and died there in about 100AD. It is to this city's church that Jesus addresses his first letter -- which makes sense because this was the grandfather church to the whole area.

The Description of Jesus

The second element in each of the letters is a description of Jesus taken from Chapter One. In Chapter One John is describing how He sees Jesus, but in each of the letters to the churches, Jesus describes Himself. Jesus says, "These are the words of him who holds the seven stars in his right hand and walks among the seven golden lamp stands." When Jesus does this, He is making absolutely sure that everyone in the church knows that these words are not from John, but from Him. John would never say that about himself! Also, these descriptions of Himself are obviously carefully chosen to describe *an aspect* of Himself that would especially impact, or be meaningful to, the church.

In this case Jesus describes Himself as "the one who is holding the seven stars in his right hand and as the one who walks among the seven golden lamp stands." We learned from the end of Chapter One that the seven stars are the "angels" of the churches, and that the "lamp stands" are the churches. When Jesus talks about the "angels" or "stars" of the churches, He is talking about the pastors, the preachers ... the leadership of the church. Jesus is specifically addressing these letters to them, so they can pass them along to the congregation.

So what was Jesus trying to get across in His description of Himself here? Well, Ephesus, as the evangelistic hub and missionary-sending church, was really the mother of all of the other churches. They were the first, and through them a lot of positive things happened in the cities around them. The surrounding cities owed their existence to God's work through the Ephesian church! But Jesus wanted to make sure that they knew their place. Yes, they were an important church, and yes, they had done some great things ... but they were lamp stands... not the light. They were flickering candles ... not the source of all light. The pastors are the stars ... but He's the one who holds them in His hand.

Yes, Jesus loves His churches. Loves them so much He died for them. The Bible says He loves His churches like a husband loves his bride ... but Jesus wants to make sure through this picture that something is clear. Yes, Jesus is walking among His church, and yes, He is showing his care by holding the leaders in His hand ... but He's the Lord of the Church and the one through whom all these things are done. He's the boss. He's the motivator. He's the person in charge in case you've forgotten.

Sometimes we get too big for our britches as a Church and we start to think that we can do effective ministry without having to bother Jesus. "Let's go do these things! What a great idea we've come up with!" we say, and we've never even checked with Jesus.

Sometimes in our individual lives we figure that we're coasting along pretty good and that we don't really need to talk to Jesus about what's going on and what we need to do. It's a deadly complacency that convinces us that we don't really need Jesus in our lives right now, and that we'll dial Him in when things get rough.

And Jesus' reminder here is that *nothing happens without Him motivating it*, whether we want to acknowledge it or not. And that everything in our life as a Christian, and in our Church, for it to be effective and purposeful for the kingdom, must be brought to Him and motivated by Him, or it will come up short.

The "I Know" Statement

The Third Element of the letters is an "I know" statement. In verse 2, Jesus says, "I know your deeds." Jesus "*knows*" what's going on in His churches ... in ALL His churches. On every board, He sits at the meeting. He's on every team. Every congregational meeting, prayer gathering, worship service, small group and staff meeting, He's there. He intimately knows what is going on in the individual lives of every single person in the church.

As the One who walks "in the midst" of His churches, and as the One who has "the flaming eyes" (1:14) that pierce everything, Jesus knows all. He has perfect knowledge of what goes on in the corporate life of the church, and He knows exactly what is going on in the individual lives of its members, right down to the motivations of their hearts and the thoughts in their heads. Nothing escapes His divine view.

Generally, in all of His letters but two, Jesus gives the good news first. I love this about Him! He's not all doom and gloom, but He encourages His churches with the good things that they are doing.

Sometimes, as a parent, I find that it feels like the only time I talk to my kids is when I'm telling them not to do something. I forget to encourage them, tell them what a great job they are doing, and how happy I am with the 25 things they've done right that day. I tend to only focus on the few things that have irritated me.

Jesus doesn't make that mistake. He knows there are a lot of good things that are going on in the church of Ephesus, and He says so. By many people's standards, this church should be a candidate for church of the year!

Jesus says in verse 2 that He sees they are "hard workers." They are not lazy Christians like the Thessalonians (2 Thessalonians 3:10-15), but are hard workers. And they have "persevered"... this word denotes being people who are brave. This church was hard-working and brave. Pretty good so far. Jesus also says that they "cannot tolerate wicked men." This church is a church that doesn't tolerate sin among their fellowship, especially in their leadership. They hold each other accountable and don't allow sin to take over their church. Another way to say this is that they practice church discipline. They aren't afraid to obey Jesus' teaching when it came to holding their people to Christian standards.

These are not namby-pamby Christians who said, "Well, just don't go around that person, he's got problems. Just don't talk about it." They are the ones who walked up and said, "You are an arrogant person and you need to repent of that." The women would walk up to the other women and say, "You're gossiping, stop it!" They'd walk up to the guy at the pot-luck table and say, "That's your fourth time through! Time to sit down." They would confront sin! (I want to say at this point that if you see me go for my fourth time through the pot-luck... I'm getting food for the kids!)

Next Jesus says, "You have tested those who claim to be apostles but are not, and have found them false." There are two ways to understand this. First, it means that they checked out believers to make sure they are true believers. They made sure that the people who *said they were Christians,* really were. It is dangerous to allow people who merely claim to be Christians to serve in the church, especially in positions of influence and leadership. They tested and checked out the Christians in the church to make sure that they lived what they professed (see Luke 6:43-45).

The second way to understand this was that they wouldn't be tricked by those people who claimed to be apostles from Jesus, who weren't one of the twelve. Believe it or not, this seemed to happen all the time. Someone would stroll into the church and say, "Right before Peter (or James or whoever) died, he had laid hands on me and has given me the mantle of the Apostle. I'm now in charge of your church and you really need to listen to me." Today we call this "Apostolic Succession." The Catholic Church, Mormons, and Jehovah Witnesses believe this; that the Apostles have passed along their authority to others. Jesus commends the church of Ephesus for not falling for this *deception.*

Jesus also commends the church for "persevering and enduring hardships for His name, and not growing weary." The Greek is in the past tense here, meaning that they had already been through it, or were on the tail end of it. This church had been through something. There was a rough patch in this church. A leader had said or done something, the government had come down on them, or some other kind of intense hardship had befallen them, *on account of being Christians*, and they had endured through it.

Long-term suffering and persecution, in one form or another, is part and parcel of being a Christian, both then and now (If you don't believe this, visit www.persecution.com and read some of the stories for yourself). And it's easy to become weary of the fight and the hardship and just give up. Jesus is honoured by us when we keep the faith, and He tells these Christians who had endured persecution and come through faithfully that He's proud of them.

The next commendation comes a few verses later in verse 6, "But you have this in your favour: You hate the practices of the Nicolaitans, which I also hate." This was a hard-working and brave church, one that resisted sin, practiced church discipline, and endured hardships and persecution well. And in addition to all this, they were strong in their doctrine.

We don't know much about the Nicolaitans, but we do know that they were professing to be part of the Christian church, and yet Jesus hates their "practices," and 2:15 tells us that Jesus hates their "teachings." Jesus commends the Ephesian church because they have seen the problems with the Nicolaitans, and they are not caught up with them. They have doctrinal and moral purity, which is so critical to a church. They can identify the people who could potentially lead them into sin, test them, and be wise enough not to let them into leadership so they will not lead the church astray.

A modern-day example of this would be the many good, bad and ugly para-church organizations that are always asking for church support. Some of them are great, like the Billy Graham Evangelistic Association or Campus for Christ, and honour Jesus and strengthen the church. But there are others out there that are simply a drain on resources, and are even dead wrong in their mission and doctrine. What Jesus is saying to the Ephesian church is that He's proud of them for being able to weed out the good from the bad based on the doctrines that they have learned from the Bible, and the trust they have in Jesus.

They had moral and doctrinal purity. It is so critical to be able to identify those people who could potentially lead us into sin, and be wise enough not to let them into leadership, or partner with us so we don't get led astray.

Christ's Church, when it is working well, accepts sinners with open arms. We love those whom Jesus loves! We go to sinners, the hurting, confused, and sick, and the trapped, addicted and depressed, and we extend the hand of grace to them and we love them like crazy. Jesus died for them, just like He did for us. Our job is not to close our doors and sequester ourselves from the world because it's full of sinners, but to invite the world in and acknowledge that we are sinners, that we hurt, and that we know about depression, we know about pain, and loss and guilt and anxiety and frustration. And above all we know the Saviour who tells us how to deal with this stuff! And we invite these people to acknowledge their own sin and mess, see where it is leading them, and to accept the Saviour into their lives to take them to the better way. They get healed and start to live their lives with purpose, peace and joy. That's how the church works when it's working well: sinners come in, saints walk out.

But among our ranks, those who are saved, those in leadership and in membership in the church, we need to be completely intolerant of sin. I hope you catch the difference there: the church is designed to help sinners, but when we focus on our members, we are completely intolerant of unrepentant, habitual sin.

When we see sin in our lives, or someone else's, we recognize that Jesus tells us to rid ourselves of the sin, and help each other destroy it. And this is not because God's some grumpy old sourpuss that just wants to rule our lives with nit-picky little rules and make us miserable. It's because He knows intimately the devastating effects of sin in local congregations, and in the lives of individuals.

We're not supposed to help each other because we love to get into other people's dirt, to point fingers and make ourselves feel bigger and more holy than others … but we get involved because we want the other person to be healthy! There should be no hint of sin among the people of Christ. Yes, we will stumble, and yes, Jesus will forgive. We forgive each other when we mess up, and extend grace, love, and peace by the bucket loads. But, a healthy church is never to be tolerant of sin.

The word tolerant here means to let the sin go on, and fester, breed, persuade, grow like a cancer and then weaken and destroy the body. A healthy church needs to confront sin, weed it out, and eliminate it; knowing that any tolerated sin will be deadly to the church.

The Diagnosis

The fourth element in Jesus' letters is the Diagnosis. With all of these great things that are going on in the Ephesian church -- good doctrine, great programs, good missionaries, full bank accounts ... Jesus says this, "Yet I hold this against you: You have forsaken your first love." At the beginning of Paul's letter to the Ephesians in 1:15, Paul commends this church for being a faithful and loving church. But now, 30 years later, Jesus looks right through all of the great deeds of the church, and sees that at the core of the church is a problem ... they had "forsaken their first love." It could also be translated, "you have lost the love you had at first" or "you don't love me or each other like you once did."

There are two important points to be made from this. First, this love was forsaken. The Greek word here is the word for being abandoned or left. They didn't accidentally lose this love, like I accidentally lose my keys, but they wilfully abandoned it, and chose to walk away from it to pursue other things. They had "forsaken their first love."

Perhaps it was the success and great ministry that had a hand in it. It's possible that because of their drive for the truth, their fierceness to stay orthodox, and their lust for being a disciplined, hard-working church, that they may have become a cold and judgmental church. Over the 30 or so years that they were doing ministry, perhaps they got so good at what they did, that they began to leave the love of people off to the side, and worse, the love of Jesus out of it altogether. What they really loved was their great and glorious programs, and their great and glorious building, and their great and glorious potlucks, and their great and glorious small groups, and they left out their great and glorious God. "You should come to our church! We won't really love you that much, but we've got a ministry you'd enjoy and a nice building."

Things on the outside seem great, but their hearts were not with Jesus, and their motivation wasn't to show love to each other ... it was for someone, or something else. One of my commentaries asks the question, "How could it happen?"

Earl F. Palmer offers this possible explanation that I want to pass along to you.

> "The Ephesus Problem happens quietly and by gradual, imperceptible shifts in focus. Let me sketch in a contemporary scenario that may explain this devastating shift of focus. What happens is that a man or woman is first united with the Christian church because of having discovered and believed in Jesus Christ

and His love. After a few years of being a Christian, that person becomes a leader in the church with very heavy responsibilities for the fellowship. But something happens along the way. That person who, because of giftedness and hard work may now stand at the vortex of church politics and decision making, experiences a subtle shift in style of life. That person is adrift as a disciple and finds himself or herself motivated and nourished by the organization or by the controversy or by ambition to hold power. The first love has been replaced while perhaps no one was aware of the replacement. The first love has been abandoned and in its place is the starchy, high cholesterol diet of activity and church work that will never nourish the human soul.

The irony of this latter condition of the "Ephesus syndrome" is that the Christian becomes totally preoccupied, fascinated by themes and goals which would have never won him or her in the first place to have joined the church; arguments over fine doctrinal points, distinctives of polity, esoteric giftedness, etc. How can this happen to us? It happens to marriages; it happens to human friendships; it happens to the life of discipleship."[i]

But the good news is that Jesus, in every one of these letters, gives a prescription to fix the problem. He diagnoses the sickness, and then like a good doctor He gives the right medicine to bring health. In this case, there are three things Jesus prescribes.

The first is in verse 5, "Remember." How do you connect with the love you had at first? Remember the way it was before you had met your love. This works in faith, in friendship, or in marriage. Jesus says, "Remember." What was life like before your true love? To Christians Jesus says, "Remember the height from which you have fallen!" Do you remember what it was like before you met Jesus? Do you know how deep in sin you were, and that you were under the wrath of God? Do you remember how far you had gone, and how far He went to redeem you? "Remember the height from which you have fallen," and at the same time, remember the depths to which He went to redeem you because He loves you.

Next, Jesus says, "Repent." (Eeek! There's that word again!) The second thing Jesus says to do to connect with our first love is to "repent." In other words, make a conscious decision to *do the opposite* of what you are currently doing. That's what repentance is. It's the conscious decision to go the other way. It's the choice to make the relationship right again.

But it's not enough just to "remember," and it's not enough just to "repent." We then have to follow Christ's third imperative: "Remember," "Repent," and "do the things you did at first." Those acts of love and devotion that categorized your relationship at the beginning ... go back and do those. In marriage this may mean going on a date, bringing flowers, giving a massage, or turning off the TV. In faith, this means doing the things that helped us learn to love Jesus. Begin the day in prayer, end the day in prayer, read the Bible daily and actually take the time to meditate on them (think about what you just read!), listen to and sing worship songs, study the life of Jesus, find new Christian friends that can breathe life into you, share your faith, take a walk in creation, do a prayer walk around your neighbourhood, join a small group or a Bible study, go to a church activity that is *not on Sunday* ... rediscover the enthusiasm of your walk with the Lord. Rediscover your first love by doing what you did at first.

"If You Don't"

The sixth element of every letter is the warning of what will happen if we don't. Jesus says at the end of verse 5, "If you do not repent, I will come to you and remove your lamp stand from its place." What does that mean? It's a terrifying concept for me as the pastor of a church, and it should be a terrifying concept for you. When a person or a church refuses to repent and turn from sin, they are wilfully promoting themselves as being outside of the Lordship of Christ. A Christian is not a Christian, and a church is not a church, unless it claims Jesus as Saviour *and Lord.*

We love the concept of Jesus as our Saviour, and we certainly should! But Jesus is also our Lord. Our boss, superior, chief, the head honcho, the motivator, and the number one. He gets to tell us what to do. And that means following His directives – doing what He says.

I love the way this is put in one of my favourite books called *Every Man's Challenge*. It was a challenging epiphany the authors gave me. Essentially they said that there needs to be a change in our minds. A change from "I'm forcing myself not to do this because it's bad" to "I'm not allowed!" This is very different than, "I have to hold on and force myself not to if I get to make the choice." The devil gets to play with that kind of thinking. He doesn't get to play with, "I'm not allowed!" That's the Lordship of Christ.

A church that does not recognize Jesus as Lord is always at risk of having their lamp stands removed. Here's the thing though; a church that has been removed can still gather, sing, and even keep doing works in the community ... but in Jesus' eyes they will no longer be His church. They will no longer be lights in the world, because they are not under His leadership and Lordship. It's been said many times, "No, Lord" is an oxymoron. If the Lord speaks, that is what we do. We refuse to be a church of Christ or a Christian when we refuse to obey Him. And part of that obedience is to be repentant from sin, and to follow with passion after our first love.

"If You Do"

The seventh element in every letter is the promise of what will happen if we do. Skip to the last part of verse 7 (not all of these elements are in the same order in each letter). Jesus says, "To him who overcomes, I will give the right to eat from the tree of life, which is in the paradise of God."

This is fairly simple, and critically important. For those who refuse to repent from sin, and who are only playing church ... their destination is destruction and Jesus will bring judgment on them by removing them from His sight. But those who repent from sin, and love the Lord are given access to the "Tree of Life." Where is the "tree of life?" Heaven, Garden of Eden, or better: where we are supposed to be. That's where we got kicked out of because of sin, and that's where we're going back to because of Jesus' work on the cross for our sakes. Those who repent from their sin, and trust Jesus as Lord, will gain access to paradise and eternal life. That's the story of the Bible, and the story of Jesus.

A church and a Christian can play church all they want. They can attend services, tithe, write curriculum, have deacons, elders, leaders, pastors, musicians, Sunday school teachers, it can battle for orthodoxy, write books, stand up against persecution, and have hard, persevering workers, and picket in front of every strip joint, abortion clinic, and porn store in the city ... and some of those are great things! But if the focus gets off of Jesus and on to anything else ... that church, or that Christian, is doomed. We can fool a lot of people a lot of the time, but we cannot fool Jesus. A right relationship with Him begins when we admit that we are sinners, when we acknowledge that we need a Saviour, and we need the Lord to rule in our lives as "the way, the truth and the life."

If the Shoe Fits

Finally, near the end of every letter is the 8th and final element. Jesus says the same thing to every church. Here He says it at the beginning of verse 7, "He who has an ear, let him hear what the Spirit says to the churches." I call this part the "if the shoe fits" part. That's basically what it means. This letter was to be read aloud to the church as they gathered together for worship. So Jesus says, "If I'm talking to you … if my Spirit is convicting you right now … if the shoe fits … wear it. Do something about it. Obey me and do what I say. Start walking in love and in truth. Come back to me off the thin ice and onto the solid ground. Listen to me, understand what I'm saying, listen to my Spirit inside of you and saying 'you need to hear this,' and obey."

CHAPTER FOUR

Smyrna: Facing Persecution

The apostle John is the writer of the book we are studying and he is writing this letter as he is in exile on the Island of Patmos. John served and worshipped in Ephesus for some time, and it was really his home church. It was also where he died in about the year 100. John was preaching and teaching there, leading people to Jesus, and so effective was his ministry that he was noticed by the Roman Government. He was found, arrested and tried as a criminal for preaching Jesus Christ as Lord. He was sentenced as a political prisoner to spend time on an island in the Aegean Sea named Patmos with other criminals. It was while he was on this island, stripped of all but the barest clothing, sleeping in the hard volcanic ground, chained up, away from his friends and his church, having to do forced labour, seeming completely halted in his ministry and effectiveness for the kingdom … that he received His vision from Jesus.

His vision has been preserved for us, and contains unique and important information for the Church and for individuals today. We as a Church can learn a lot about what Jesus expects of us, and we as individuals can hear and be convicted by critical principles of Christian practice, faith, how to live, how to face suffering, how to get to know Jesus better, how to set our priorities, and what to be encouraged about and hope for today. Most of all, I want to hear Jesus speaking to us through these letters. These are not dead letters, but ones that can affect us in our day-to-day living.

We are now going to take a look at the second letter of Jesus to the next church in Asia Minor, a church in the city of Smyrna. And again, we are going to look at it through the same matrix that we did in the last chapter.

So, if you haven't done so already, open up your Bible and read Revelation 2:8-11. I'll wait here... No, no, I'm fine, thanks for asking.

The Address

Done? Ok. "To the angel of the church in Smyrna write..." This letter is addressed by Jesus to the pastor and church in the city of Smyrna, which is one of the relatively few biblical cities that we could actually go and visit today. It is the next city the letter carrier would take along the Roman Road. Today it is found in the country of Turkey, and is called Izmir, which is the Turkish way of saying Smyrna. If you wanted to, you could go and visit the Christian church in the city of Smyrna, the great-great-great... grandkids of the church that Jesus is writing to. It is still a beautiful city, though it has lost some of the splendour and notoriety it had during the days of John the Apostle, when this letter from Jesus was written.

The city of Smyrna is considered by some scientists today to have been the most beautiful city the Greeks ever built. It was first founded in the year 1000 BC, and was then destroyed by the Persians in the 545 BC. Sadly, the city lived as a shadow of its former self for over 200 years until the time of Alexander the Great. He conquered the land and commissioned one of his generals to rebuild it in about 300 BC.

Old Smyrna was founded on a small hill, but the new ruling order had a greater vision for it. They moved the site of the old city to the slopes of Mount Pagos. One source says that "the flat-topped Mount Pagos seemed destined by nature to be the acropolis"[ii], or outside wall, of a great and beautiful city.

It was because of the location on Mount Pagos, and the city founded around its summit, that it became known as the Crown of Smyrna. Ships approaching from the sea would look up at the mountain and the large buildings and great wall would look like an enormous crown.

The city, set on the sides of the hill and sloping into the sea, was surrounded by the beauty of nature, and was the site of some of the greatest architecture of the day. In the city were a huge library, a great stadium, and the largest public theatre in Asia. There were also amazingly ornate and beautiful temples lining the famous "Golden Street."

Smyrna was not only known for its beauty and wealth, but also for its patriotism. If you were to ask the Roman citizens of the day how they felt about Rome, almost all of them would reply with euphoric joy, saying how proud they were to be citizens of the greatest nation in the world. It was that pride that escalated into worship of the empire.

I know this feeling because I'm a Canadian. We aren't given much press for our patriotism, but I'll put a maple leaf waving, maple syrup slopping, beer drinking, Hockey Night in Canada watching, snow shovelling, wheat producing, beef eating, fish catching, Tim-Bit eating Canadian up against a patriotic American any day. Canada was rated the number one country to live in according to the UN Human Development Index for 10 years in a row until 2001, and only slipped to 6th in 2006 (I suspect it has something to do with Tim Horton's changing their baking policy). And on Canada day, or when the winter Olympics is on, Canada is abuzz with patriotic fever.

If there were Roman sports jerseys and antenna flags in Roman times, they would have been up all year! However, in ancient Rome, the passion didn't stop at patriotism. When the worship of the empire became full grown, it became not only worship of Rome, but worship of the one who ruled Rome and personified her ... the Emperor.

At first, the emperors resisted being worshipped as gods, but as you can imagine, it wasn't long until they relented ("Well, okay, you can worship me"). And then it not only became a way to be patriotic, but it *became law.* If you were a loyal citizen of Rome, by law, you would have to worship the Emperor in a special ceremony at least once a year by entering the Emperor's Temple, burning a pinch of incense, drinking some sacrificial wine or eating some sacrificial meat, and saying, KAISOR CURIOS, "Caesar is Lord." After that you could go on with your peaceful Roman life.

In 26 AD, while Christ was living a quiet life in an obscure part of the empire called Nazareth, there were many large and important cities that were bidding for the opportunity and privilege to build the Great Temple to Caesar Tiberius. Imagine the benefits and patriotic pleasure of having the Emperor's temple in your town!

We still have some of the coins that were minted in Smyrna, and some still bear the mark of pride that Smyrnians had in their city. They called themselves the "First City of Asia." They proclaimed themselves as the most loyal Roman city, and because of it, were given the right to govern themselves. Smyrna was chosen above all others to build the great temple because of its patriotic loyalty. The city became the centre of emperor worship, sometimes called the Imperial Cult.

There were a large group of Jews, or Jewish converts, living in the city of Smyrna. They were the only ones who were exempt from emperor worship because of the ferocity with which they had fought with the empire during the Great Jewish Revolt in 66 AD. No one else in the empire was exempt but them.

It was in this remarkable city that the church was planted. We don't know how it happened. There is no historical record of it, and the New Testament is silent, but we do know of it from Paul's three-year stay in Ephesus when he was setting up his evangelistic centre. The scripture mentions in Acts 19:26 that Paul had been ministering and doing missionary work in many parts of Asia, and probably had set up the first church in Smyrna. Probably either he, or someone he trained, established this church.

As you may have guessed, it was difficult to be a Christian in Smyrna, the most patriotic city in the empire and centre of emperor worship, where each year every citizen had to declare that Caesar was Lord. This presented great problems for Christians who believed that Jesus was their only Lord.

Any sports fan who has worn the opposing team's jersey during a live game knows this. If you would like to feel a portion of the tribulation that the Smyrnians went through then just do this: If you live in Alberta, buy a Calgary Flames jersey, hat and foam finger, then walk up and down Whyte Ave after a game. Or alternatively, buy a Toronto Jersey, hat and foam finger and watch the game at a Sports Lounge in Ottawa. You'll get a taste of a Smyrnian Christian's life.

The "I Know" Statement

Here we get a flavour for the kind of life that Christians in Smyrna led. Jesus says, "I know your *afflictions* and your *poverty*—yet you are rich! I know the *slander* of those who say they are Jews and are not, but are a synagogue of Satan."

The Christians in the church of Smyrna were not bad citizens (I've heard that there are some very nice Calgary Flames fans...). In fact, many historical writers say that the Christians were good citizens, and innocent of any crimes. One author says that Christians were known as good tax payers and loyal citizens, that they made no trouble, and helped the poor and needy of the day.[iii] But the problem with the Smyrnian Christians was that they refused to worship the Emperor as Lord.

The book of Acts tells the story of the first Christian martyr. His name was Stephen, and he was persecuted by the Jewish ruling class for being a follower of Jesus Christ in the year 35 AD. By the year this letter from Jesus was written, in about 90 or 95 AD, persecution of Christians had grown tremendously, and had become an empire-wide problem.

The real persecution of Christians under Rome began in 64 AD when Nero blamed Christians for the Great Fire in Rome … a fire that most people believe he started. Nero claimed Christians to be enemies of the empire, and began ferociously singling out and mistreating Christians, even to the point of torture and murder. Nero was known to throw garden parties and at these parties he would take the Christians that he had been torturing, douse them in oil, tie them to a wooden stake, stick them on a pyre, and use them to light his gardens at night.

By the year 90 it really began to catch on that reporting Christians would gain you favour with the local Roman government. In fact, if you reported your neighbour as a Christian, and that Christian refused to burn the pinch of incense to the Emperor and say "KAISOR CURIOS," you could claim a portion of the martyr's possessions after he was killed. It was a bonus to turn in the Christians.

The martyring and suffering of Christians actually became a popular pastime and public "blood sport" for Romans of the day. Just as there are extreme sports, reality shows and the X-Games today, they had their version back then.

The greatest extreme sports of the day were the gladiators and public displays against the barbarian invaders. They would be caught and herded into the arenas to do combat. The sports heroes of the day were the gladiators who would battle these enemy barbarians or each other … to the death. If you've ever seen the movie Gladiator, you'll know what I'm talking about.

The problem came when there weren't enough enemy barbarians to send into the arena to fight. So the next logical solution was to take the Christians and send them into the arena with the gladiators, instead of just torturing them to death. They wouldn't put up much of a fight, if any, but they would settle the bloodlust of the up to 87,000 fans gathered to watch the games in the various arenas and coliseums.

But, human nature is to push everything to the extreme. Killing Christians became as popular as hockey, football, basketball and baseball is today. It was especially dangerous to be a Christian during the time of the great Roman Games. Sending Christians up against gladiators wasn't enough for the crowds. So they started sending them into the arena up against wild animals like boars, bears, and even lions that would be starved for days and would tear the person limb from limb. One church Father named Turtullian said that "they were constantly inventing new outrages [against the Christians], as if they were taking part in a prize competition [for who could inflict the most pain or spill the most blood]."

To refuse to burn the pinch of incense and claim "KAISER CURIOS" was to risk being thrown in the arena, imprisonment, torture, and death. Christians were often crucified upside down and then left to starve on their crosses or be eaten by wild animals.

Each area of the empire seemed to have a favourite method for dispatching Christians. In Arabia they were known to kill Christians with axes. In Macedonia Christians were hung by their feet above a fire until they were asphyxiated. In Alexandria the locals' favourite method was to cut off the nose, ears and hands of the Christians and let them die. In Antioch they were roasted to death. In Thebias they would be dragged naked over broken pottery, conch shells and the heads of spears until they were torn to shreds, and then fed to wild beasts. In Pontus they were known to drive reeds under the fingernails of the Christians, pour molten lead on their backs, tear off their private parts, spill their stomachs and leave them for the dogs.

The "lightest of punishments" that a Christian could hope to face was to have their right eye hacked out with a sword, to have their left foot branded with fire so they would be crippled, and then to be condemned to toil in the Roman copper mines for the rest of their lives.

Christians were beheaded, boiled in oil, and had anchors tied around their necks to be drowned. In the year 303 AD everyone in the town of Phrygia in Asia Minor, except the Roman mayor and his magistrates, were burned alive in their homes because they would not renounce their faith in Christ and say the two words, "KAISOR CURIOS." This was the daily life and fear of the Christians of Smyrna. This was the reality that they lived with every single day. This was the reality that came when they claimed Jesus as their one and only Lord.

It was to a church like this that Jesus wrote, "I know your afflictions and your poverty ... I know the slander..."

The word "afflictions" is the Greek word THLIPSIS, and is the word for "pressure." Jesus says, "I know the extreme pressure, the tribulation, and the affliction that you are under." It was constant, daily, unrelenting pressure to give up their faith, to renounce Christ and to walk away from the threat of torture and death that loomed over them always.

We think we know pressure? Most born and bred North Americans know nothing of pressure. For people like me, the pressures of life are often those that I bring on myself because I am too greedy, foolish, selfish and stupid. The Christians of Smyrna knew real pressure.

They also knew poverty. Jesus says, "I know your afflictions and your poverty." There are two words in the Greek for poverty. The word PENIA and the word PTOCHEIA. The word PENIA is the word used for a person who is just getting by. They are not wealthy and are living, what we would call "month to month," barely able to keep food on the table ... just scraping by. That's PENIA.

Jesus here doesn't use the word PENIA, He uses the word PTOCHEIA. This is the word for absolute and total destitution, extreme poverty, and miserable living conditions. This church wasn't just under persecution, they were also under sanctions by the people of the community. They were literally starving to death in one of the wealthiest and most beautiful cities in the ancient world. Because they would not claim "KAISOR CURIOS," no one would trade with them or hire them, and once someone was found to be Christian, they would be fired. It was dangerous and costly to claim Jesus as your Lord.

Jesus also says that He knows "the slander of those who say they are Jews and are not, but are a synagogue of Satan."

There was a large population of Jews, or Jewish converts, in Smyrna and they were actively opposing the Christians in the city. They felt that belief in Jesus Christ as the Son of God and Messiah of Israel was in insult to them. It was offensive to even look at a Christian for them. Christianity disgusted them.

The preaching of the Christians was that salvation was found in Jesus Christ, the suffering Messiah who had come to take the punishment for all mankind. And that because of His work and teaching, the Law was fulfilled and there was no longer a need to be circumcised, abstain from certain foods, or obey the whole law of the Old Testament Torah … and the Jews were incensed by this. The Christians even had the nerve to study and learn the Jewish Bible and call it their own.

They would sell out the Christians at every turn, would promote the sanctions against them, and as Jesus said, would "slander" them. They would accuse them, fight with them, and took great pleasure in their mistreatment and torture, which Rome was more than happy to dole out.

I just want to pause here for a minute and point something out. Jesus says, "I know" here. There's something special about that word that we don't get by reading the English version. It's more than intellectual knowledge. Not like how most of us "know" about the suffering of children in Africa, or we "know" about the destruction of cities in Malaysia, or the hurting children of Chernobyl. When Jesus says, "I know" he uses the word OIDA. John Macarthur in his study says, "The Greek word for 'know' is *oida*. It means, 'I know by experience,' not 'I know by observation.' Jesus is not observing them; He knows what is happening by experience."

A counsellor is so much more effective when he or she has experienced what the other person has gone through. If you come to me for addiction or abuse counselling, I can't really help you. I can give you some Bible verses and point you in the right direction, but I don't know what it's like to go through that kind of pain.

But there are some people who are amazing addiction counsellors, and superb abuse counsellors, and by and large it's because *they've been there*. They know by experience the pain of withdrawal, or a fist from a lover, and therefore they can walk with you. That's the word that Jesus uses here when He says OIDA.

Does Jesus know, by experience, the difficulties of financial poverty? Yes, the Bible says Jesus was poor. Does Jesus know the fear of imminent death? Sure He does. Does He know the afflictions of torture and of losing loved ones to the hands of others? Absolutely. Does Jesus know what it's like to be slandered, to be abused verbally, accused falsely, brought before a twisted court, and then sold out to be chained up, tortured and killed? Yes. Hebrews 4:15 says that "we do not have a high priest who is unable to sympathize with our weaknesses, but we have one who has been tempted in every way, just as we are—yet was without sin." That means … *Jesus has been there*. Not just observing what you and I have gone through … *He's gone through it too*.

Are you feeling afflicted today? Do you know the frustration of poverty? Are you slandered and accused? One of the greatest differences with Christianity is that our Lord and Saviour is not far from us, merely observing our lives from an ivory tower or gilded palace. Jesus knows by experience how we feel.

That's why we can talk to Him about it, and how we can know that He is our best advocate as the one who "is at the right hand of God and is also interceding for us" (Rom 8:34). He stands by the Father and says, "I know what this is like, so Father, please shower down mercy on them. I know what this is like." He sympathizes with you. He empathizes with you. And "He knows your afflictions."

The Description of Jesus

Move back up to the end of verse 8, the part that describes Jesus. Jesus' words about Himself at the beginning of this letter say that, "These are the words of him who is the First and the Last, who died and came to life again." Right from the outset of the letter He wants the Smyrnians to know who is writing. He is someone who knows.

He was there at the beginning of all life, of *their* lives, and of their suffering: He is the First. He will also be there at the end of their suffering, at the end of their lives: He is the Last. Jesus tasted death, He is the one "who died." He wants them to remember that He knows life and death by experience, and that He not only knows death, but He is the One who also came to life again. He conquered death, and has experienced the resurrection Himself.

This church and its people had been beaten down on every side, and were on the verge of being snuffed out for good. They needed the reminder that Jesus really is alive, is sovereign, has perfect knowledge of what they are going through, and that even though it looks bleak for now, He knows how they feel and is in control of the outcome. He has the power to pass along hope and new life to them, and there is nothing that takes Him by surprise. Even if the believers suffered to the point of death, the One who, as Jesus said before in Chapter One, "holds the keys of death and Hades," will raise those martyrs to new life again with Him. These people needed hope, and the knowledge and resurrection of Jesus was that hope.

The Diagnosis

The fourth part, the Diagnosis, is fairly simple to see. The diagnosis is that this is a suffering church. This church is suffering, dying, starving, shrinking, and losing hope. But this church's diagnosis includes a piece of important information.

Jesus says, "Do not be afraid of what you are about to suffer. I tell you, the devil will put some of you into prison to test you, and you will suffer persecution for ten days." Who is putting them in prison? The devil. Look at verse 9. Whose synagogue are these slandering Jews in? The "synagogue of Satan."

Part of this diagnosis that Jesus is giving is to tell the church not to get so focused on what is happening to them that they lose sight of the larger battle.

When a patient comes into the doctor's office, they usually come in with various "presenting symptoms." Things that have gone wrong with the body that are visible or experienced by the patient. Then these "presenting symptoms" point the doctor towards the root cause of the problem. Yellow skin equals failing kidneys. Large black spots on skin could mean cancer. Pain in the abdomen could mean appendicitis.

In the same way, these sufferings that the church of Smyrna was under were "presenting symptoms" of a larger problem. There was a larger battle, a spiritual reality to their suffering. They needed to understand that they were a part of this battle. Ephesians 6:12 reminds believers that, "Our struggle is not against flesh and blood, but against the rulers, against the authorities, against the powers of this dark world and against the spiritual forces of evil in the heavenly realms." Peter warns us in 1 Peter 5:8 that, "Your enemy the Devil prowls around like a roaring lion looking for someone to devour."

Unlike other churches we will look at, Jesus does not have a problem with the church of Smyrna. This is one of only two letters that are full of commendation and encouragement. Jesus wants these believers to know that their persecution and poverty, the pressures they are under are not a result of judgment against them, as they may have wondered, and perhaps as the local Jews were saying to them. They may have wondered, "What have we done to deserve this?" or "Perhaps the Jews are right when they say that God is judging us." "Maybe we need to change something, to compromise." Jesus says, "No, it's not something you have done or need to change in your life! You are where you need to be. You are a soldier. You are being attacked because you are part of a greater spiritual war."

When they joined the Kingdom of Heaven, they set themselves against the Kingdom of Darkness and made themselves enemies and targets of the Devil.

The Prescription

Jesus, in the midst of his diagnosis, also gives his prescription. He says, "Do not be afraid of what you are about to suffer. I tell you, the devil will put some of you in prison to test you, and you will suffer persecution for ten days. Be faithful, even to the point of death." What are His two prescriptions for the church of Smyrna to last throughout these trials, tests, and troubles?

Do not be afraid, and be faithful. It almost seems trite, doesn't it? When I first read these words I thought, "What? That's it? Really?" Seems like something you'd embroider on a pillow, or hang on a wall under a picture of flowers, or write on a card to send to someone you don't really know! Not something that is supposed to sustain me or anyone else under this kind of persecution. Too easy words for an impossibly hard situation.

But then I remembered that these are the words of Jesus, and that I'd better pay closer attention and look deeper at them. These are the words of Jesus to all those who are facing hard situations.

In effect He says, "If you know Me, you can trust Me. If you trust Me, then you realize there is a greater perspective on the situation. If you realize the perspective I have, and the power I hold, then you know that I hold the keys to death and Hell. If you know the hope of eternal life with Me ... then you do not need to be afraid."

In Matthew 10:28 Jesus gives a very pointed, sobering teaching by saying, "Do not be afraid of those who kill the body but cannot kill the soul. Rather, be afraid of the One who can destroy both soul and body in hell." There is only One Being that needs to be feared. And it is not the slandering Jews, not the opposing government, not the torturer, the gladiator, the one who fires you from your job, the parent, spouse or anyone else that is making your life a living hell. It's not even the one behind it all – the Devil. The only one that needs be feared is the One who holds the keys to death, hell, and eternal life. And if you are in good stead with Him ... then there is ultimately NOTHING to fear!

Jesus says, "do not be afraid," and also "be faithful, even to the point of death." All these Christians had to do was to light a little pinch of incense and say two simple words, "KAISER CURIOS" and they would be released to trade, work, raise a family, and live peacefully. But Jesus commands the Christians to "Be faithful." One bishop called that pinch of incense, "the freedom that brought a curse with it."

Jesus faced the same temptations in the desert. He knows. The Devil stood in front of Him and tempted Him to give up the cross, the torture, the rejection and the pain; to walk away from poverty, the frustrating disciples that will break His heart, the religious leaders who would ridicule, and all the rest of the trouble that would come during His life. The Devil said, "all you need to do is bow down to me and I will grant you the whole world. No need for torture and death. Just a simple bow of the knee and all would be over."

Jesus knew this temptation, and He also knew the consequences. He knew there would be no payment for sin and salvation for the world if He did not suffer the cross. Jesus looked at Satan and said, "Away from me, Satan! For it is written: 'Worship the Lord your God, and serve him only.'" Why? Because He is the only One that need be feared. Again ... Jesus knows what the church is going through, what we are going through. And He passed the test to show us how.

"If You Do"

Part six of every letter is the promise of Jesus "If you do." Let's read verses 10 and 11, "Be faithful, even to the point of death, and I will give you the crown of life. He who has an ear, let him hear what the Spirit says to the churches. He who overcomes will not be hurt at all by the second death."

If we do overcome the temptation to deny Christ (which, if we are honest with how serious Jesus takes sin, comes daily), to bypass the frustration that comes with standing up for our Christian convictions and the word of God, and endure to the end, then Jesus gives us two promises.

First, that He will give us the "crown of life." Smyrna was famous for its athletic games. And the greatest prize was the crown that would be won by the greatest athletes. The crown was a wreath of flowers, or a garland that would be placed on the head of the winner of the games, the one that endured the pressure, the fight and the hardship of competition and walked away the victor: they would receive the crown of the Romans. Those who won the crown were known and praised as great citizens and patrons of the empire. Jesus gives the same promise to those who endure. They will gain the crown of eternal life, and they will be known and praised as great citizens of the Kingdom of God. The Victoria Cross, or Medal of Honour of Heaven.

The next thing that Jesus promises to those who overcome is that the Christian "will not be hurt at all by the second death." What is this second death? Hell. I encourage you to read Revelation 20:7-15. This is almost the end of the Bible. Jesus is cleaning house, He's done with evil, and those who would be saved are saved:

> "When the thousand years are over, Satan will be released from his prison and will go out to deceive the nations in the four corners of the earth—Gog and Magog—to gather them for battle. In number they are like the sand on the seashore. They marched across the breadth of the earth and surrounded the camp of God's people, the city he loves. But fire came down from heaven and devoured them. And the devil, who deceived them, was thrown into the lake of burning sulphur, where the beast and the false prophet had been thrown. They will be tormented day and night for ever and ever.
>
> "Then I saw a great white throne and him who was seated on it. Earth and sky fled from his presence, and there was no place for them. And I saw the dead, great and small, standing before the throne, and books were opened. Another book was opened, which is the book of life. The dead were judged according to what they had done as recorded in the books. The sea gave up the dead that were in it, and death and Hades gave up the dead that were in them, and each person was judged according to what he had done. Then death and Hades were thrown into the lake of fire. The lake of fire is the second death. If anyone's name was not found written in the book of life, he was thrown into the lake of fire."

This is what Jesus was talking about. Those that stand up and remain faithful to Him, even to the point of death on earth, will not taste the second death in eternity. They will not be in danger of Hell. In Matthew 10:32 Jesus says, "Whoever acknowledges me before men, I will also acknowledge him before my Father in heaven. But whoever disowns me before men, I will disown him before my Father in heaven." Those who *really* believe that Jesus Christ is *really* the Son of God and *really* is the One who holds eternity in His hands, and can *really* save a person from the eternal torture of Hell … will not be swayed by the threats of any human being.

"If You Don't"

We may think that we have great prizes, crowns, treasures and security in this life, but what does it matter if our eternity is not secure? Jesus once said, "What good will it be for a man if he gains the whole world, yet forfeits his soul" (Matthew 16:26). Everyone will experience the first death. It could be quietly in sleep, glorious in battle, alone in a hospital, or martyred for faith. Everyone will face the first death. After that, everyone will also face the judgment seat of Christ. Everyone will be resurrected and stand before His throne. And they will be judged for their actions, and their faith will be found out.

Those that endure faithfully here in this life will be resurrected and brought into eternity in paradise with Jesus. We cannot say this enough as a Christian Church. Those that deny Christ and refuse to live for Him will be sent to the second death, the eternal separation from God and His love in the torments of Hell. This is eternal death. If this isn't important to understand, nothing is. If this isn't a motivation to talk to people about Jesus, then nothing is.

Does this mean that Christians don't feel the pain? Of course not! Christians don't deny the pain of torture, or loss, or grief. We don't try to live in denial of things that are bad in this world. Too many times well-meaning Christians will walk up to someone who is hurting, maybe even at a funeral, and say, "So, are you rejoicing in the Lord today?" "Isn't it great that this happened?" That's ridiculous. It's foolish! Christians don't deny that life hurts sometimes, and we don't deny needing time to mourn or get angry or frustrated, to punch a pillow or cry into one. What it means to be a Christian is to put all these things into perspective. Life hurts, but inside that tempest and storm ... we have an anchor. That Jesus loves us, knows where we are, and holds our future securely.

We don't know many names of people who were pastors of churches in the time of the Apostles. But we do know who the pastor of the church in Smyrna was. He was a man named Polycarp. Pastor Polycarp. He was born in about 70 AD, in the days of the Apostles, and studied under the apostle John. When Jesus addresses this letter to the "angel of the church in Smyrna," he is most likely addressing it to Pastor Polycarp.

At age 75, in the year 155 AD, Pastor Polycarp went to visit Rome. When he returned to his church in Smyrna, he had the misfortune of returning during the time of the great festival. Part of the festival was to be great sporting events in the arena. What happened to Pastor Polycarp that day was actually sent around in a letter from the church in Smyrna so everyone would know.

Eleven Christians had been put to death by lions during the festival, but the bloodlust of the people continued to run high and the crowd longed for a fresh kill. The cry was raised out by the crowd, "Let us search for Polycarp!" As pastor of the church, he was known to the community and they wanted him to face the lions.

Polycarp, at first, was persuaded by his friends to run away to a local farm-house, from the pursuing soldiers that came to bring him to the arena. When they found the farmhouse the soldiers tortured two of the farm boys until they gave up Polycarp. Escape was still possible, but the old man refused to run any more. He met the soldiers as they came to get him and asked them to wait while he had a short time of prayer. They allowed it, and Pastor Polycarp actually ordered food for the soldiers while they waited.

It was then that the soldiers brought him before the Proconsul, who tried to get Polycarp to deny Jesus Christ. He said, "Swear by the fortune of Caesar. Take the oath and I will release you. Curse Christ!"

Polycarp stood firm saying, "Eighty and six years I have served the Lord Jesus Christ, and he has done me no wrong. How can I blaspheme my King who has saved me?"

Hearing this, the onlookers in the arena demanded that the lions be loosed on him then and there.

"Swear by the fortune of Caesar," the Proconsul insisted.

"If you vainly imagine that I will swear by Caesar, and pretend that you do not know who I am, listen plainly. I am a Christian," Polycarp replied.

"I have wild beasts," the Proconsul warned. "If you do not repent, I will have you thrown to them."

"Then let them come, for my purpose is unchangeable," Polycarp said.

"If the wild beasts do not scare you, then I will order you to be burned alive!"

"You threaten me with a fire which will burn for an hour and then go out, but you are unaware of the fire of the judgment to come, and the fire of eternal punishment which is kept for the ungodly. Why do you delay? Bring on the beasts, or the fire, or whatever you choose; you shall not move me to deny Christ, my Lord and Saviour."

When the Proconsul saw that Polycarp would not recant, he sent the herald to proclaim three times in the middle of the stadium, "Polycarp has professed himself a Christian."

As soon as they heard these words, the whole multitude of Romans and Jews furiously demanded that he be burned alive. It was Saturday and Jews ran out of the arena to gather timber and scraps of wood, breaking their Sabbath laws so they could watch the Christian burn alive.

Polycarp was bound and placed on top of the pyre. "This is the teacher of Asia," the crowd shouted. "This is the father of the Christians, this is the destroyer of our gods, this is the man who has taught so many no longer to sacrifice and no longer to pray to the gods."

Pastor Polycarp looked up to heaven and prayed, "O Father, I thank you, that You have called me to this day and this hour, and have counted me worthy to receive my place among the number of the holy martyrs. Amen."

As soon as he had said the word "Amen" the officers lit the fire. The fire burned around him, rising high above his body, but seemed to burn away from him. Then someone called for a soldier to finish him off quickly with a dagger, and Polycarp was stabbed to death and left to burn. The pastor of Smyrna died as many of his people had done before. (I'm not sure for copyright purposes if you need to cite where you found the quotes from this story)

If the Shoe Fits

"He who has an ear, let him hear what the Spirit says to the churches." What is Jesus saying to you as you read this? Is your future and eternity secured in Jesus Christ? How have you been facing your persecutions?

How have we denied Christ for the sake of the ease of our life, and the shame of being called a Christian in public? When you first began your walk with the Lord Jesus, did someone sell you some kind of easy street Christianity, or are you aware of the spiritual reality around you, and that there is a war that all of humanity is part of?

The words, "Do not fear" are sheer and utter madness in this world … there is much to fear … unless there *really* is a God, who *really* did raise Jesus from death. And because He did, there is a new version of truth, and a new vision victory in this world, and a new reality in which we can live. We live in hope, and we need not fear.

CHAPTER FIVE

Pergamum: Flank Attacks

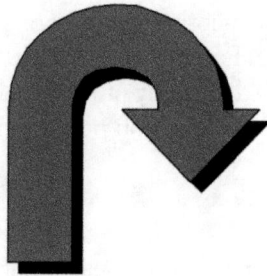

I don't know much about military strategy or what the best placement of troops would be during a battle, but I've seen enough movies to know that you don't take all of your soldiers and send them all in the same direction, on the same offensive. Some need to go one way, while others go another. Some cover the frontal attack, others the flank, and still others stay behind in reserve for backup. I also learned that you don't send in all your soldiers with the same weapons, or they might compromise their effectiveness if the enemy has a counter defence. You need multiple weapons and multiple strategies to win a war.

Satan knows something about waging a war too. He's been watching and doing it for a long time. In the churches that we've studied so far, and that we will continue to study, we have seen different attack strategies launched against each of the churches.

In Ephesus, the attack came more intellectually, more quietly, and from the inside of the heart of the church. Satan tempted them, effectively, to forsake their first love, to cool their hearts, and to love the "starchy, high cholesterol diet" of church work, or themselves, or other things, more than Jesus.

In Smyrna, the attack was far more transparent. It was a physical, brutal, outside attack where the cruelty of Satan was absolutely poured out on the Christians. The attack came from outside forces, like the Jews slandering the church, and the Romans physically assaulting, arresting, imprisoning, torturing, and killing them.

As we look at Christ's letter to the church in Pergamum, we will see a different attack pattern. In each church Satan's end goal is the same; he wants the people to stop worshipping Jesus as Lord and to stop telling people about Him as Saviour. That's the goal, and he uses multiple attack strategies to accomplish it. In Pergamum, Satan doesn't concentrate his hit from just the front … he tries to win the war by attacking from the side: the flank assault. What Jesus calls, "the attack of Balaam." Someone once said, "Satan doesn't care which side of the boat we fall out of. His only concern is to make us fall."

So, this is the point where you go get your Bible again, open it up and read Revelation 2:12-17. I'll wait here… Got any chips or pretzels to share?

The Address

Done? Ok, let's take a look at Pergamum.

After leaving Smyrna, the letter carrier would have continued his journey along the coast of the Aegean Sea, taking the Roman Road about 40 miles north along the Caicus River. About 10 miles inland stood the impressive capital city of Pergamum. Some Bibles will have the name as Pergamum, others will have "Pergamus," some might even have Bergama. All are the same word: Pergamum is the neuter form, and Pergamus is the female form, Bergama is the current name of the city.

Pergamum, the capital city of Asia, was built on a hill about a thousand feet above the surrounding countryside. The name of Pergamum actually means "citadel," and must have been what the city looked like in the day, a great citadel reaching far into the sky.

Pergamum rivalled Ephesus as the leading city of the region and, as the capital, had become the centre of Asian culture. A contemporary example of this might be Ottawa in Canada, the centre of Canadian culture.

Pergamum, like Ottawa, was a sophisticated city, full of many urban features that we have today. It had a large theatre that sat about 10,000 people. There was an enormous library, the second biggest in the world, only bested by the famous library in Alexandria, Egypt. The library of Pergamum didn't contain a lot of books the way we know them; it was full of scrolls. It had over 200,000 scrolls, held in little boxes and cubby holes in the walls and shelves of the library. In fact, it is from the name of this city that we derive our word "parchment." And behind that word is a great story.

The story goes that at one time the library in Pergamum tried to lure away from Alexandria one of their best librarians. Something like, "C'mon over to us, we'll give you a better health care plan, more helpers, a nice house, and all the KFC you can eat."

The King of Egypt was so upset that he stopped exporting papyrus, a type of paper made of water reeds that were abundant in Egypt. Papyrus was what almost all scrolls were made of back then. "You try to take our librarian! How dare you! No paper for you!" (Please note the failed Seinfeld reference... I'm sorry.) Because of this embargo, Pergamum had to come up with a different kind of paper to write on, and they invented parchment, made from dried sheep and goat skins (Eww.). This was an inventive, intelligent, and creative city.

Pergamum was also the centre of worship for four idolatrous cults. Four of the most "important" gods of the day: Zeus, Athene, Dionysus, and Asclepius. The chief gods of the city were Zeus and Asclepius. Both were symbolized by the serpent. Asclepius' symbol was the coiled snake, a symbol you've no doubt seen before.

Asclepius was the Greek god of medicine and healing, and his temples functioned somewhat like modern-day hospitals. People would pilgrimage for many miles to come to Pergamum to worship in the temple of Asclepius, to receive treatment from the doctors, and a blessing from the priests, seeking miraculous healing. Many doctors today still use the coiled snake of Asclepius to identify themselves as doctors.

The Description of Jesus

It is to this city that Jesus says, "These are the words of Him who has the sharp, double-edged sword." This is especially poignant since the proconsul, the governor or military commander of the province had the rare power known as "the right of the sword," meaning he had the political power to judge a party guilty, and then perform executions, even of Roman citizens and military men, without having to check with Rome first.

Jesus tells this church that though this Roman official, in their home town, had the right to try and execute prisoners, his power was only temporary, and only bound to the flesh. Jesus is the one who holds the true, "sharp, double-edged sword."

Again, as with all of the other images of Jesus, this comes right from Chapter One. The sword was Rome's symbol of authority and judgment. In the same way, Jesus uses the image of the sword to let the church know that it is He who holds the final judgment. Jesus has the ultimate power over life and death, not the Roman official.

Throughout scripture, the Word of God is symbolized by the sword. I have, in gold letters inscribed on the cover of my Bible, the words, "Big Al's Sword" to remind me of my fiercest weapon.

In Ephesians 6:17 Christians are told to take up the "sword of the Spirit which is the word of God," our only offensive weapon. Hebrews 4:12 probably has the best picture of the power of the Sword of God. It says that "the word of God is living and active. Sharper than any double-edged sword, it penetrates even dividing soul and spirit, joints and marrow; it judges the thoughts and attitudes of the heart."

Pergamum's proconsul may have had "the right of the sword" given by Rome, but he had no power over eternal life, over where souls end up, and the destiny of the person after death. That judgment, the truly important judgement, which will be perfectly rendered, is reserved for Jesus alone.

This was not only meant to be an encouraging thought to the individuals in the church, but a sobering one as well. We'll see in a moment that Jesus had a problem with this church … with people's choices and their allegiances. They needed to remember that what they did, the choices they made, and the lives they lived, would one day be judged by the One who holds the double-edged sword. And that it will be judged by a standard, and that standard is the word of God. They need not fear the judgments of humans, but there is a judge to be feared, and everyone will meet Him one day.

The "I Know" Statement

Next we move to the "I know" statement. Jesus says "I know" two things. First, He says, "I know where you live—where Satan has his throne … where Satan lives." I've said this many times before, but it can't be over emphasized: Jesus knows our circumstances.

Are you ever driving or walking around your neighbourhood or city, and suddenly come to the realization of what kind of world is surrounding you? Do you ever feel like you live in Satan's city (no, I don't mean Calgary)? Or work at Satan's job-site? Maybe you look around and wonder if Satan rules your neighbourhood? Maybe you feel like Satan has taken over the airwaves, TV and newspapers, because everything seems tainted? Have you ever taken a walk or driven downtown and taken a look at the stores that line the streets, and wondered if there is anywhere that is pure anymore?

Pergamum had its issues too. Everywhere you went you were surrounded by pagan symbols, some very lewd, very graphic sexual symbols. Pagan temples and idols to Roman and Greek gods were everywhere. Even the government that you lived under was ruled by a pagan emperor and a religion that made it illegal not to worship the emperor as a god. Jesus knows where we live and sees the spiritual reality of where we are.

Second, Jesus says, "I know… you have remained true to my name. You did not renounce your faith in me, even in the days of Antipas, my faithful witness, who was put to death in your city…" He says, "I know where you live, the situation around you, the temptations you face, and the hurts you are feeling. I know where you live, but I also know that despite it all, you've been faithful to me."

This church lived in a tough city, but they were not giving up their faith. They continued to believe in Jesus Christ as the Saviour of the world, and to believe in His death, burial and resurrection… even though they were being persecuted for it. It was not easy to be a Christian in Pergamum. Daily pressure to deny Christ; ridicule from friends, neighbours, family, government and the Jews; ostracism of the people who called them "atheists" (because they didn't believe in the Roman pantheon of gods) and who told them they were unpatriotic fools, bad citizens, and bad Romans.

The people of this church stood firm, even during "the days of Antipas." Who was Antipas? His name means "against all," and he was one of the members of the church who did stand "against all" of the people who wanted him to deny Christ, and was martyred for his faith during a time when persecution was especially bad.

According to a 10th century legend, Antipas was brought before an image of Caesar and told to confess that Caesar was God. When he refused, the Roman official said, "Antipas, don't you know that the whole world is against you?" (Not a new argument… "C'mon! No one believes that!" A close cousin to "C'mon! Everybody's doing it!") He replied, "Then Antipas is against the whole world!" Antipas was then placed inside a brass bull which was heated with fire until he was roasted to death.

There are other ancient traditions which suggest that the name "Antipas" is a symbolic name (or a nickname) for Timothy. Notice that Jesus gives this martyr the same title as He gave Himself in 1:6, "the faithful witness." Even during that difficult time, in that difficult city, under so much pressure, surrounded by temptation, Antipas and the rest of the church held fast to the name of Christ as the resurrected Lord, and were faithful witnesses.

The Diagnosis

But Jesus has a problem with this church. His diagnosis says that though the church had been successful in being faithful during the frontal attacks, the persecution, and pressure to deny Christ, Satan was attacking them on their flank, where they weren't looking, and the church was in danger of losing the battle.

Jesus begins in verse 14, "Nevertheless, I have a few things against you. You have people there who hold to the teaching of Balaam, who taught Balak to entice the Israelites to sin by eating food sacrificed to idols and by committing sexual immorality. Likewise you also have those who hold to the teaching of the Nicolaitans."

We've talked about the Nicolaitans before, so I don't want to retread that ground, but the illustration that Jesus uses in regards to Balaam is quite important.

Balaam's story is found in Numbers 22-25. For Pergamum, Jesus is almost certainly not referring to an actual person named Balaam, but is speaking of someone around the church who was doing the same thing there that Balaam had done to Israel many years before.

Balaam is the one whom the Israelites credit with instigating idol worship in Israel. He was a pagan prophet, a sorcerer, who said that he could influence the gods for or against someone by his special incantations and offerings. Of course, he did this for a price; the god's will goes to the highest bidder.

King Balak was the king of the Moabites, and was getting quite nervous about this large group of Israelites who had just come marching into his territory after leaving their captivity in Egypt. So he went to the sorcerer Balaam and paid him to pronounce a curse on Israel. He was going to wage war on Israel, but to hedge his bet he figured that he'd get

Balaam to sway the God of Israel against them. At first Balaam didn't want to, but King Balak made him an offer he couldn't refuse.

So Balaam tried to work his magic on the God of Israel, and tried to pronounce a curse on them, but God kept putting blessings in his mouth. Three times, in three different places, Balaam tried to curse Israel, but each one came out a greater blessing than the last. King Balak was frustrated that the sorcerer couldn't do the job, especially since he had paid him so much, and all he got was a series of blessings on an enemy army. So Balaam decided that he would go about it a different way. We learn in Numbers 31:16 what that other way was. Balaam basically said to the Moabite King, "If you can't curse them, corrupt them."

Now we turn to Numbers 24:25. After the final accidental blessing, scripture says in Numbers 24:25 that, "Balaam got up and returned home and Balak went his own way." So they split up, seemingly defeated. But we learn in the beginning of Chapter 31 that Balaam came back to the king after some time and gave him a new plan. And it basically went like this:

"Ok, here's what you gotta do: Take your most beautiful women, married or not, and send them into Israel to entice and have sex with the men and soldiers of Israel. Tell them that if they want some more, they can come to the pagan temple in Shittim and sacrifice to the god there, that they will get to have even more sex with the even more beautiful women there, and the temple priestesses."

Numbers 25 tells us how it happened: "While Israel was staying in Shittim, the men began to indulge in sexual immorality with Moabite women, who invited them to the sacrifices to their gods. The people ate and bowed down before these gods. So Israel joined in worshiping the Baal of Peor. And the LORD's anger burned against them. The LORD said to Moses, 'Take all the leaders of these people, kill them and expose them in broad daylight before the LORD, so that the LORD's fierce anger may turn away from Israel.' So Moses said to Israel's judges, 'Each of you must put to death those of your men who have joined in worshiping the Baal of Peor.'"

We start to get a taste here of how serious God takes sexual sin, and how powerful these flank attacks are. We also get an idea here of what Christ means when he says to Pergamum in Revelation 2:16, "Repent therefore! Otherwise, I will soon come to you and will fight against them with the sword of my mouth." But we're not there yet.

The sin of Pergamum was eerily similar to that of the sin of Balaam. They had stood strong against persecution, but what Satan could not accomplish from the frontal attack, he tried to do from the side. Jesus' problem with the Pergamum church was that they were not standing out from the world as a holy and set-apart people any more, but were letting sin and worldliness fit into the church and individual lives, and it was undermining people's relationship with Him. Did they still believe in Jesus as Saviour? Yes, they did. They had their theology mostly straight. But the people of the church were corrupting themselves by joining in temple worship, indulging in sensual parties, and committing acts of idolatry and paganism.

Now we may think today, "Well, that can't happen to us, there are no pagan temples around for us to go to, and there are certainly no temple priestesses that we are temped by." No? In many ways the side attack of Satan, the same one that he used in Pergamum, is as dangerous today as it was then. Jesus didn't rebuke this church because they were compromising their faith, but rebuked them because they were compromising their relationship with Him! *They still believed in Jesus,* and got straight A's in Sunday school … but they were failing miserably at the practice of their relationship. They still went to church and believed in Jesus … they just didn't take their relationship with Him all that seriously.

Compromise involves the blending of two different ideas. I want to do one thing, you want to do another. "I want to go to Burger King, you want to go to Wendy's, why don't we go to both and take the food to the park? Let's compromise." Sometimes compromise is a good thing, and helps build relationships. Not in this case.

Believers, Christians, should cooperate and participate in society whenever we can. Paul says we are to be good citizens, and Jesus says we are to be "salt and light" in the world. We are to flavour the world, add to the world, and shine our light all over the city. People should know that when they walk into a Christian church and ask for help with a civic project, or something else, that the church is always willing to help. Our cities should be spilling over with gratitude because we are such good servants of our home towns. We are to be "in the world," as in, we are to interact, help, care for, enjoy and minister to the people of our world … our county … our city … our neighbourhood … our home. But we are not to live like the world.

Romans 12:2 says that we are not to be "conformed to this world." While Christians are supposed to participate in city and community matters, we also need to remember that we are separate, holy, and set apart from the world as well … because many things in this world are dangerous and sinful, and will compromise our faith and relationship with Jesus.

2 Corinthians 6 says it this way. Eugene Peterson's THE MESSAGE BIBLE reads:

> "Don't become partners with those who reject God. How can you make a partnership out of right and wrong? That's not partnership; that's war. Is light best friends with dark? Does Christ go strolling with the Devil? Do trust and mistrust hold hands? Who would think of setting up pagan idols in God's holy Temple? But that is exactly what we are, each of us a temple in whom God lives. God himself put it this way:
>
> 'I'll live in them, move into them; I'll be their God and they'll be my people. So leave the corruption and compromise; leave it for good,' says God. 'Don't link up with those who will pollute you. I want you all for myself. I'll be a Father to you; you'll be sons and daughters to me.', The Word of the Master, God."

Christians, while serving and loving the people of this world, praying for our enemies, caring for the sick, teaching people, and helping the hurting ... we need to avoid any partnership, participation or practice that may lead to immorality or sin. I know myself, and maybe you are like this, I imagine that if the government would turn against Christians and start persecuting them, or if people decided they were going to chase us down and harm us for our faith, that I would never turn against the Lord!

We often look, expect and even brace for the frontal attack, and figure we're OK. We say, "I'm not tempted in that area." We look at other fallen believers and say, "I'd never do that! How can they do that?" We think ourselves to be fine and strong in the frontal attacks, when all along we are leaving the flank open.

We say we have no temptation to murder someone or physically assault them ... but the flank is wide open ... we are tempted to hold our grudges, to not give forgiveness, to gossip about the person, and to treat them like dirt. It's not murder, but Jesus says it is sin just the same.

We have no temptation towards some sexual sins like rape, practicing homosexuality or molesting a child, and we are horrified by people who do those things ... but then Satan comes from the side. He tempts us to fill our minds with sexual images, stories and humour, with pornography, false ideals of how relationships should be, to be insecure with our bodies and to try to hold ourselves up to some kind of sexual ideal. He tempts us in our fantasy life and in our language. That's sin too, and it compromises our ability to have a right relationship with Jesus.

Skipping church is not a temptation for some people (I'm not one of them). It doesn't even cross their minds. But Satan attacks in a different direction. He keeps us too busy to take a Sabbath rest each week, keeps us from opening and reading the Bible during the week, he encourages us to fill our minds with distractions so that we can't pray, concentrate or meditate. He convinces us that we are far too busy to share our faith, visit the sick, be there for our kids or our parents, to have friends over, to visit the neighbour or pray with our spouse.

We may think that Satan is conquered in many areas of our lives, just like the Pergamum church did, but what we don't see is that he's really winning the war—not from the front, but from the sides.

The Prescription

So what is Jesus' prescription for these flank attacks? It's pretty simple. When those who call themselves Christians succumb to these side attacks and compromise their relationship with Him, Jesus says, "Repent, therefore."

Listen to the Holy Spirit prompting us to recognize it as sin, and repent. Repentance means to stop doing it (or start doing it if it is a sin of omission), turn around, and start going in the other direction, fixing the mess that we created on the way back.

I've got a great illustration that makes repentance easier to swallow. Say you're trying to get from your house to your buddy's house in the next city. And say, you are directionally challenged like me (I once got lost in my basement and had to live on mislaid Cheetos and popcorn I found under the couch cushions until my wife came and found me).

You get into your car and start to drive, but at some point you realize (when you begin seeing polar bears and igloos) that you may be going in the wrong direction. So what needs to happen?

First, you have to realize you're going the wrong way. Acknowledging the "sin" (Greek HAMARTIA, "to miss the mark") is the first step in repentance. It sounds simple, but for many, this is a step they don't want to take because then they have to (*shudder*) admit they were wrong.

Second, you have to stop the car. In other words, stop "sinning." It doesn't help the cause much if you acknowledge you're going in the wrong direction, but don't do anything about it. Throw out the magazines, turn off the internet, stop making those phone calls, pour out the bottle, smash up the package, toss out the chips ... STOP IT!

Third, turn the car around. This is the true meaning of the word "repent" (Greek METANIOA, "to change one's mind"). It's not enough to stop the car; it has to be turned around. This puts legs to what has been acknowledged as sin. Many people say that stopping is enough. Nope, now it's time to turn around. This means not facing the direction of the sin. Not going to that place, deleting those e-mails, cancelling that subscription, walking away from those conversations...

Fourth, start going the right way. Check your GPS, call your friend, pull out the map, and check the compass ... find the right direction and *start moving towards it!* It's not enough to turn the car around and not go anywhere. Real repentance means moving the car in the right direction as well. Start reading the scriptures, going to church, attending the small group, talking to friends, get some good books...

Fifth, and this step is often forgotten, undo the false turns that you've made. On the way back you will have to undo many of the turns that you made wrongly to get you back to the right road. This means going back to the people you have harmed by your sin, undo the lies and gossip you've told about others, give back what you've stolen ... MAKE IT RIGHT!

God promises in scripture that He rewards those who persevere in lives of holiness, where we turn from sin and turn to Him, away from compromise and toward full-commitment.

"If You Don't"

Jesus says, if you don't repent, "I will soon come to you and will fight against them with the sword of my mouth." What does that mean? A couple things.

It means that the time for repentance is now! Jesus says, "I will soon come..." Jesus' letter is addressed to the whole church, but He's really talking to individuals within it. He's talking to those who fell for the side attacks ... and also to the rest of the church who let this happen to their brothers and sisters.

Jesus under-girds the call to repentance with the threat of imminent judgment. Is it a threat? You bet it is! If this church, and the individuals therein, don't recognize their problem, ask forgiveness, repent from sin and turn back to Christ, they will find out that they will meet Jesus far sooner than they expect, and will be judged far quicker than they imagine.

Often, people, Christians and non, think that they will have their fun, put off dealing with their sin problem, and deal with it later. For many, "later" comes way too soon and they find themselves standing before Jesus, being judged for what they have done, and it's too late to repent.

In 2 Corinthians 6:2 Paul says, "I tell you, now is the time of God's favour, now is the day of salvation."

Why am I hammering this point home? For two reasons. First, because there are some people that are reading these words who figure that they are going to coast along in life and not make the committed decision to become fully devoted followers of Jesus until later in life. They may be believers, or not, but there are things they want to do, habits they don't want to give up, and things they know that Jesus is going ask them to deal with that they just don't want to be too uptight about. And so they are putting it off. I want to warn them that putting off this decision and telling Jesus to "get lost for now" will be the worst decision they'll ever make.

And second, because too many Christians have become far too lax in the practice of their faith, and far too much like the world. And I'm guilty of it too. For every finger I point here, I know that there are three pointing back at me. I know that I'd much rather spend the night watching a movie, and the morning sleeping in, than commit that time to doing something that I know Jesus wants me to do. I'd much rather sweep my marital and relational problems under the rug than confront them openly and honestly. Many times I'd much rather spend time reading my favourite books and educating myself than reading books to my kids and putting the work into teaching them the things of God. There are lots of ways that I allow the side attacks of Satan to cripple the possible relationship I could have with Jesus, and the potential blessing He could bring in my life if I'd only do things His way. God help me.

"If You Do"

For those that do overcome, those that do repent and turn back to Jesus, or turn to Jesus for the first time, Jesus says at the end of verse 17, "To him who overcomes, I will give some of the hidden manna. I will also give him a white stone with a new name written on it, known only to him who receives it."

There is a lot that could be said here, but let me just hit the major points. There are 3.

First, the Hidden Manna. For those who turn to Jesus, who have been trying to feed themselves with the world's goods, and find that it does not fill or satisfy them … Jesus says he will give them the "hidden manna," the food reserved for those who believe in Him … the "Bread of

Life," Jesus Himself. Those who refuse to eat at the feasts of the pagans and are sick and tired of the listless, bloated, sick, McHangover that comes with the indulgent, fatty, garbage food of this world, are not really missing out on anything because they will be given better food that will truly satisfy; the Word of God and a personal relationship with Him built on forgiveness, grace, peace and joy.

Second, the White Stone. There is much to say, but not much is known about what exactly Jesus meant by "the white stone." Certain kinds and colors of stones were used for various purposes in the ancient world.

Some were worn around the neck as a special good luck charm. Some were used like food stamps are used today. Others were used as tickets or invitations to special events and parties. In the courtroom, black and white stones were used by juries to cast their votes of guilty or not guilty.

Whatever idea that Jesus had in mind here when He said that He will "give him a white stone," the main idea is that those who have repented and sought right relationship with Him are at that point *included*.

Sometimes it's hard to be a Christian and be different from the world. It's hard to have different priorities from other people, avoid certain places and practices that others indulge in, to always seek to take the moral high ground, to live the servant's life, and to usually walk around looking a little bit weirder than most other people. But that's the calling of the Christian. This is why Peter, in his first letter, calls Christians "aliens" and "sojourners" in this world (1 Peter 2:11).

Jesus says, "Yes, you will look like an outsider in this world, but remember, you will belong to me, and be included where it really matters, in Heaven, in the kingdom of God." I'm not the kind of guy who's going to be able to walk up to any of the clubs in town and get past the red-felt rope guarded by the seven-foot-tall bouncer ... but Jesus says that as I turn to Him, repent of my sin, and live a life devoted to Him, that He will grant me the ultimate back-stage pass... the white stone that allows me access to eternal life with Him in Heaven.

Third, Jesus says that He will grant "a New Name." Where the Hidden Manna represents the new food and sustenance found in Jesus, and the White Stone represents inclusion in His kingdom when we feel like outsiders, the New Name represents the new character and person we become as God works in our hearts.

This either means that our new name (or our new character) is that of Jesus Himself, or it means that our new name is a special name, a specially designed character, personality, and destiny, hand-crafted by

God, and given by Jesus to us. Both work for me! The name of Jesus branded on my heart and life, or a destiny so intimate and special that only God knows it, and He's willing to share it with us as we grow deeper in our relationship with Him. A name so powerful that knowing it will change the course of our lives forever.

If The Shoe Fits

So, "He who has an ear, let him hear what the Spirit says to the churches." What is Jesus speaking to you? Do you have any secret sins in your life where the flank attacks of the enemy are compromising your walk with Jesus? What is the Holy Spirit saying right now? Maybe you need to put down the book and deal with some things with Him – right now. Alternatively, have you repented and asked Jesus to be your Lord and Saviour for the first time? Do you want the Hidden Manna, the White Stone, and the New Name for your life?

So much of the world is in the church, and so many churches look just like the world that sometimes it's hard to tell the difference. So many Christians are in the world, and so many Christians are just like the world that there is no difference between them and their lost neighbour. Being a Christian, a follower of Jesus, sets us apart. Are we ready to live that way?

CHAPTER SIX

Thyatira: Compromised Morality

I think, of all the churches Jesus writes to, I understand Thyatira best. I grew up in a place very similar to it. Hinton was, and is, a trade city. Wood, pulp and coal are what my home town is all about. Most dads there are tradesmen, and when I was growing up, most of them were union guys. My dad was a union man for almost my whole life. When I would come home from college, I too would join the union, pay my dues, work at the pulp mill, and gain the privileges and responsibilities of being a union brother.

Anyone who has ever worked in a union factory with skilled tradesmen knows that a certain subculture forms - unwritten rules of conduct, relationships and ways of dealing with others that are not in the union manual. You learn terms like "scab," a non-union worker who takes a union guy's job. It was not only bad news to be a "scab" in Hinton, it was potentially dangerous. During the strike, I remember being warned about places in town that it would be "better if I didn't shop there." I remember the garbage men in town stopped picking up garbage at the houses of those who worked for the company, and were non-union. It was especially troublesome for those people who were working for the company, and were in charge of negotiating the new contract with the union. Cars scratched, threats made, friendships ended.

If you were in the union, toed the line and respected the rules (written and unwritten), you would be fine, even prosperous. Families of union guys would stick together, go fishing, hang out after work, party, and be around each other all the time. If you worked the twelve-hour shift, you spent far more time with the union brothers than you did with your wife and kids. Consequently, most of the men were divorced, and pornography and swearing (what they called "industrial language") was commonplace. If you picked up a magazine, it was probably Maxim, FHM, Playboy, or Sports Illustrated. If you were playing cards, or saw someone playing solitaire, it was more than likely that the cards had nude women on them. After a hot day, or a long shift, most of the guys didn't go home, they went to the bar, the strip club, or threw an ad-hoc party, BBQ or something else together, always with alcohol, and they sometimes got quite carried away.

Being a Christian, going to a "Bible College," and doing my training as a pastor, kind of made me stick out from this crowd (much like the way a neon flower-painted 1960's VW Bus would "stick out" in the parking lot of a Nine Inch Nails concert). I worked hard to do my job, but I worked harder not to swear and to avoid the magazines, posters and other stuff around the area ... I opted instead to read Spider-Man comics or the Bible. Temptations abounded, and I succumbed often, especially in the first few years.

As I grew closer to Jesus, it became harder to avoid situations where I would offend people, become defensive, or just look like a Bible-thumping weirdo. More than once I found myself in a conversation or situation that I would have preferred to crawl away from than to finish ... often it was 10 to 1 against. I don't know if you've been there, but it's not as fun as you might think.

So, if you haven't done so already, go get your Bible again and open it up and read Revelation 2:18-28.

I'll wait here. Dum-de-dum… Hey, ever see that episode of Star Trek where … oh, never mind.

The Address

Done? Great! My predicament in Hinton was very similar to that of the Christians in Thyatira, though they also had the Roman government constantly breathing down their necks and threatening to kill them. Thyatira was a union town too. Back then, they didn't call them "unions," but "trade guilds."

Thyatira was not built on a hill like the other cities we have looked at. It was situated in a valley, 20 miles from either Pergamum or Sardis along the Roman Road. Because it was in a valley, it didn't have a natural defence, so they had a large garrison of soldiers that protected it, almost another kind of "guild."

With all of the trade guilds there, Thyatira was a major manufacturing centre. Cloth making, leather working, pottery, and metal working were especially popular. Thyatira was also famous for its bronze working and its legendary purple-dyed cloth.

If you remember the story of the Philippian church, you will remember the first group of people Paul met there. The story is found in Acts 16 where Paul comes across a group of women worshipping God by a local river. One of these women, Acts 16:14 says, was "a woman named Lydia, a dealer in purple cloth from the city of Thyatira, who was a worshipper of God."

Lydia's trade was dyeing, someone who stained cloth. She was particularly well-known for her purple cloth (actually a deep-red color – go figure), which was a very special and expensive commodity back then. The guess is that Lydia worked and lived in Thyatira, but came out to Philippi so often to sell her cloth that she bought a home there too. It was in her second home that Paul started the first church of Philippi. Lydia was most likely an integral factor in the planting of the church in Thyatira.

There were no important temples in the city, but of course emperor worship was still commanded, and Apollo was worshipped as the guardian of the city at the Greek Temple of Tyrannus.

The problems that Jesus addresses later were directly tied to the trade guilds. If you've ever played any games like Ultima, Everquest or World of Warcraft, then you already know a lot about trade guilds (and are probably a nerd). Most people in Thyatira's trade guilds were not warriors or mages though … they were regular, blue-collar tradesmen who belonged to one trade guild or another.

Each area of the city had its own hall, which was the centre of the guild's activities. Not just work-related stuff, but civic meetings, training, socializing and worshipping was also done in the guild halls. Each week there would be a banquet in the hall with lots of food, a party atmosphere, and a place where the trade families could have fun and connect after a week of hard work. The parties centred around socializing, but they were also a time of worship of the guild's patron god. They would serve meat sacrificed to idols at the party, and would drink together. Though it was not meant to be an orgy, and it was generally frowned upon to descend into total debauchery, there was some sexual license given, and the parties sometimes got out of hand.

It was not *necessary* to be in a trade guild, but it sure made life easier. Just like when I was growing up. If you wanted to get and keep your job, to be around friends, to make new friends when you came into town, or if you wanted to have any kind of a social life in Thyatira, it really helped to be in a guild. To not be in a trade guild of some kind made you a social outcast.

If you were found out to be a Christian, which would probably happen quite quickly when you stopped worshipping the guild's god, stopped drinking too much, started being faithful to your wife, and stopped messing around at parties … you were in trouble. The society would label you a "hater of the human race," kick you out of the guild, stop dealing with you professionally, and report you to the Roman authorities.

It was to this church that Jesus writes because there was someone in their midst that, though she sounded like she was teaching right and smart things to do, was leading the church into sin and evil. She had some thoughts about how to circumvent all the problems with the guilds. She was Jezebel, and we'll talk about her later.

Description of Jesus
In verse 18 Jesus uses three phrases to describe Himself to the church of Thyatira.

First, He calls Himself, "the Son of God." This would be especially interesting to the people of Thyatira. The Emperor of Rome, whom all Romans were obliged to worship as a god, was considered to be an incarnation of Apollo, the protector of Thyatira. Apollo was the son of Zeus, the chief god and Helios, the sun god.

The phrase that Jesus uses here is only found once in the book of Revelation. Jesus seems to be making the point to Thyatira that though everyone around them worshipped Apollo as their guardian, and as the son of god … Apollo had no true power to save, and was merely a dead idol and a false god. It was Jesus who was the true Son of God. He had proved it by His miracles and flawless life, by buying their salvation, and by rising from the dead.

Second, Jesus says His "eyes are like blazing fire." Move down to verse 23. Jesus is there pronouncing judgment on those who follow the false teaching of Jezebel and says, "then all the churches will know that I am He *who searches hearts and minds*." That's what Jesus means when He says His "eyes are like blazing fire."

I want you to get two pictures of fire in your mind. First, a raging forest fire. Nothing stands in the way. No obstacle can block it, no barrier can stop it. It drives around lakes and jumps rivers and highways, removing every obstruction in its way. There is nothing that can block the view and the ferocity of the perfect perception of Jesus.

The second picture is a welding torch. Intense fire, under control, able to cut and pierce metal, flesh, stone and bone. The piercing eyes of Christ that search the hearts and minds of all people can be likened to the intensity of a welding torch.

Jesus says that He knows our "hearts"; He uses a word that speaks of our rational mental process, the thought progression behind our actions. God knows exactly how we came to *that decision*.

The word "mind" is actually the word for "kidneys," believed at the time to be the centre of human will and intentions. Jesus doesn't just see the actions, but the mind's process by which we came to those actions, *and the intentions* behind them. He knows if we are working hard or slacking off … and he knows if our deeds are done for selfless or selfish reasons, no matter what they look like to others.

Third, Jesus says He has "feet of burnished bronze." Bronze represents strength for exacting judgment. If you look again to verse 23 it says, "I am He who searches hearts and minds, and I will repay each of you according to your deeds." The perfect, piercing, all-seeing eyes of Jesus allow Him to pronounce perfect judgment on the righteous and the unrighteous. Revelation 14 speaks of the harvest of all the people of this world who are not found in Christ. They are gathered up and trampled under the feet of God.

The idea here for us, and those in Thyatira, is that Jesus is the true Son of God. He sees all that we do, knows our actions and the intentions behind them, and will judge everyone according to His irreproachable, perfect judgment. Those who remain faithful, but look oppressed, are known by God. And those who look good on the outside, but are full of evil intentions and greed on the inside, who have not submitted themselves to Jesus, will eventually be discovered and judged for who they really are.

The "I Know" Statement

To this church in Thyatira Jesus next says, "I know your deeds." In other words, "I know what's going on in your city, in your church, in your guilds, and in your lives." One great thing about these letters from Jesus is that most often He starts with the good news, some encouraging words for the church. There are five things about the church that Jesus sees and applauds them for.

First he sees their "love." This church is the opposite of Ephesus. Ephesus had been standing up for doctrine, and had identified false apostles and teachers properly ... but they had lost their first love. They were a cold church. Thyatira, on the other hand, was full of loving people. So loving, in fact, that Jesus congratulates them for it. Love for each other, love for others, and love for God. But their love had morphed into a bad kind of tolerance. I would call that kind of tolerance, "love out of control." They loved each other, but they ended up also loving the false teachers among them, and their teachings, and their followers, rather than dealing with them as Jesus wanted them to.

Second, Jesus mentions their "faith," or faithfulness. They were steadfast holding to the story of the gospel, the story of Jesus and of Him as their risen Saviour.

Third, they were encouraged for their "service." This is the same Greek word for our word "deacon": DIAKONIA. They were a church that acted like good deacons. They visited the sick, fed the hungry, gave to the poor, supported the widows, took care of the families, visited the prisoners and cared for the orphans. They were a good, serving, loving church.

Fourth, they were commended by Jesus for their "perseverance." The fact that they still existed at all in that hostile environment was a testimony to their perseverance in the face of persecution.

Fifth, Jesus says, "and that you are now doing more than you did at first." This was a maturing church. They were growing spiritually, they were serving more people, they were loving more people, and they were enduring more than ever. They were maturing as individuals and as a church.

The Diagnosis

But, or "Nevertheless," Jesus says, "I have this against you." In this great, growing, loving, faithful, maturing church ... there was a cancer growing. This church was a beautiful body on the outside, but was dangerously close to death on the inside. The membership looked great, but they were about to fall apart. The piercing eyes of Jesus saw through to the core. Like an X-Ray or an MRI, Jesus examined the inside of the body of the church and found a huge ball of disease growing.

David Jeremiah says this in his study of this passage: "[At this point in the letter] the tone changes. Outward conduct may be exemplary, but we can't fool Him. His burning eyes pierce the darkness and flash with the flame of moral anger."[iv]

We've already talked about flank attacks, the blind-side attacks of Satan. This was another. John Stott says, "If the devil cannot conquer the church by the application of political pressure or the propagation of intellectual heresy, he will try the insinuation of moral evil. This was the dragon's strategy in Thyatira."[v]

Jesus explains more in verse 20, "You tolerate that woman Jezebel, who calls herself a prophetess. By her teaching she misleads my servants into sexual immorality and eating food sacrificed to idols."

Who was this Jezebel, and what was she teaching? Well, this "Jezebel" was probably not named Jezebel at all, just like the trouble maker in Pergamum was probably not named Balaam. This is most likely a way for Jesus to show the church what was happening, by showing them the same story in scripture.

Jezebel's story begins at the end of 1 Kings 16, after verse 29, when we read about King Ahab, the future king of Israel marrying the very beautiful pagan Philistine, Princess Jezebel. Her name is synonymous with evil.

The Jews consider her to be the most evil woman to have ever lived. She helped the Israelite King Ahab to do, what scripture says, "more evil than all the kings before him." She introduced King Ahab, and all of Israel, to Baal worship, and even encouraged him to put an altar to Baal in the temple, right next to God's (It's important to note that Jezebel didn't try to replace the God of Israel, but to add another god along side Him).

She also encouraged him to put up worship sites called Asherah poles where Israelites could go to indulge in religious prostitution and idol worship. The Bible says that Ahab and Jezebel "did more to provoke the Lord, the God of Israel, to anger than all the kings of Israel before him."

Jezebel would hunt down and kill the prophets of God, and sacrifice them to Baal in bloody rituals to try to break the drought that God had prophesied through Elijah. Baal was supposedly the god of the rain clouds, and the God of Israel used a drought to showcase Baal's impotence, and His strength. In fact, Jezebel killed so many priests and Israelites that she almost single-handedly destroyed the house of David.

The worst thing that Jezebel did though was to introduce sorcery, magic and sexual pagan idol worship to Israel. The chosen people of God were rejecting Him and instead indulging in temple prostitutes, sexual sin, and worshipping dead idols alongside the living God. In effect, they were worshipping demons and their own flesh rather than the God who had rescued them from slavery in Egypt, and who loved them dearly.

Thyatira had a woman like this in their midst. A powerful, influential, beautiful woman who was teaching something that compromised the worship of the church, and their relationship with Jesus. A good argument could be made that this was the pastor's wife, and that she was the one teaching falsely, but whatever the case, she was a Jezebel.

Her greatest threat was that she had a ready-made solution to the problem that the Christian members of the trade guilds had, those who were afraid of loosing their jobs and livelihood because of their faith.

She seemed to have two main teachings. Both of them were very persuasive. The first was what we might call *toleration*. She argued and taught that it was all right to tolerate, and even join in during the guild banquets, even eat the meat and join in on the sexual side of the party.

"After all," she may have argued, "Jesus saves your soul, and is only truly interested in your faith. He wants you to believe in Him, worship Him and serve Him … keep doing that, but there's no reason why you can't do the other things as well! Serve Jesus, love God, and have fun at the guild parties. Jesus wants us to be good citizens, right? Well, it's our civic duty to attend these gatherings. Jesus wants us to share our faith, right? Why risk friendships over these little parties, or little sex things? Isn't being with our neighbours and telling them about Jesus more important? Why alienate everyone! God gave us these bodies to enjoy ourselves, right? And Jesus has saved our souls, right? So let's enjoy ourselves at the guild banquets. After all, meat is just meat, right? Even Paul and Peter say that. Even if that meat is sacrificed to idols."

Persuasive? Certainly! Tempting for the people of the church who were under attack and duress? Absolutely.

The second of Jezebel's teachings is found in verse 24. Jesus says, "Now I say to you in Thyatira, to you who do not hold to her teaching *and have not learned Satan's so-called deep secrets....*" This was Jezebel's second ploy and false teaching. And we've heard it before. We'll call it *indulgence*. She may have been teaching that in order to defeat Satan, one has to enter His stronghold.

Perhaps she said something like, "How can we know good if we do not know evil? How can we know the seriousness of commitment, if we do not know the temptations of liberty? How can we know the deep things of God, and truly appreciate His love and grace and forgiveness, if we don't understand the deep things of Satan, sin, sexuality, indulgence and evil?"

In a twisted way, it kind of makes sense, right? But that's where the trap is set, and where Jesus steps in.

The Prescription

Jesus' prescription is the warning against this type of slippery slope argument. Jesus calls her "misleading." Like a false treasure map, meant to lure people away from the real treasure, Jezebel promises to lead the believers one way, but misleads them to another.

She was a false teacher, with persuasive words, who was a member of the church, was gifted, talented, beautiful, intelligent, successful, sexually liberated and very attractive. That, and she was alleviating a lot of pressure and tension with her teaching. She was saying that it was OK to indulge in the booze and sex, things that many people struggle with. She was also saying that it was fine to compromise the worship of Jesus, because "Jesus understands our unique, difficult situation, and doesn't mind some concessions for the sake of making life easier. He would never expect his people to choose suffering, would he?"

Remember, she called herself a prophetess of God ... so she supposedly *spoke for God.* The bottom line was that she was enticing believers with moral compromise, twisting the words of the Bible, leading people away from Jesus, and convincing them to worship something other than God alone.

Our sin is not usually something we see as bad, dirty or unattractive at first ... or else none of us would sin! Sin is attractive, it fulfills a desire, it is persuasive, seems right at the time, knows exactly what we want, and is smoothly seductive.

Like the worm in the apple, sin is hidden behind the rich, red, shiny exterior ... it's not bold, nor does it often advertise itself as sin. It's not until we take a bite that we feel the sickness.

It won't convince you to dismiss God. It won't try to tempt you to walk away from everything that is good and right in this world. That's too much. What it'll do is simply ask you to nudge off a few degrees ... just a little bite ... one try ... a quick look.

"Don't stop worshipping God!" it says. "Don't stop going to church, don't stop loving your wife, don't stop going to work ... just add this little bit to it." And that little bit spreads like a drop of grease on our finger. Soon it covers our hands, and more and more ... the slope gets slipperier and the consequences begin to pile up.

Any sin tolerated *will* take over a person and make him or her ineffective and weak. Any sin tolerated by a church *will* take over a church, and make it ineffective and weak. Any sin tolerated by a society *will* take over that society and make it ineffective and weak. Look around and ask if tolerated sin doesn't spread and weaken if it is not cut off and cut out.

"If You Don't"

Again, as with almost every one of these churches, the prescription is repentance. Jesus says, "If you don't repent ... if you don't cut off and cut out this cancer of sin ... this Jezebel, then this disease is going to spread throughout your church."

Jesus says in verse 21, "I have given her time to repent of her immorality, but she is unwilling. So I will cast her on a bed of suffering, and I will make those who commit adultery with her suffer intensely unless they repent of her ways. I will strike her children dead. Then all the churches will know that I am He who searches hearts and minds, and will repay each of you according to your deeds."

For Jezebel, it was too late. She had her time, she was warned, and Jesus was patient with her, but that patience has ended, and she has caused enough damage. She won't repent, so Jesus has to cut her cancer out of the church. Jesus, as He always has, deals harshly, fiercely and decisively with sin. He loves this church and the people inside of it too much to allow them to be trapped and damaged by this sinful teaching any longer.

For those who follow her, even share her bed, Jesus says that they will be cut off and cut out too if they do not repent. Those who persist in following her, those who Jesus metaphorically calls "her children," will be destroyed along with her. This sin gets no more toleration. This cancer cannot be allowed to spread any farther, and Jesus, the Great Surgeon must deal with it … all of it. This toxic slime covered and corrupted the pure gospel, misled the people in the church, and therefore needed to be dissolved and removed.

Jesus was angry with Jezebel, but He was not much more impressed with the church that had tolerated her and her slippery slope teaching. He gave them time to identify the problem, to deal with it, to repent … and He even forestalled judgment, but the problem needed to be dealt with. Mercy is only temporary for those who choose to hold on to their sin (read that last sentence again). I hope you understand how serious God and Jesus take sin…

"If You Do"
Verse 24 says, "Now I say to the rest of you in Thyatira, to you who do not hold to her teaching and have not learned Satan's so-called deep secrets (I will not impose any other burden on you): Only hold on to what you have until I come."

Remember, *this was a good church*, but it had a large problem. Jesus' first promise was to "not impose any other burden" on them. Once the problem was dealt with, once the cancer was cut out, the healthy body could keep going and keep doing what they were doing well!

Jesus' second promise for those who do repent and for those who are faithful is in verse 26. "To him who overcomes, and does my will to the end, I will give authority over nations—He will rule them with an iron sceptre; He will dash them to pieces like pottery — Just as I have received authority from my Father."

For those who do repent, and who do commit to the lifetime of obedience until the end, Jesus says that He will grant them "authority over nations." He reminds them of the prophecy of Psalm 2 that was all about Him. Go read Psalm 2 in your Bible. No seriously, go read it.

What we read there are the words of God spoken to the Messiah. God, through the psalmist, writes this letter to His Son Jesus, and allows us to read it so that we will know that the future reign of the Messiah will be shared with the faithful. How great is that?!

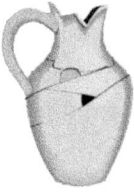

The imagery of the "iron sceptre" and the "pottery" is taken right out of Psalm 2. They symbolize total judgment and total victory. This church was compromising because they were worrying that they would lose too much by defying the guilds. Jesus tells them by following Him, yes, they will lose something in this life, but they will *gain everything in the next.* They will share in the total victory, and they will be spared the destructive judgment that will be brought down on those outside of a relationship with Him.

People in ancient days would write the names of their enemies on clay pots and then smash them to bits to symbolize their victory. Where do we want our name written? On the white stone we talked about last chapter, reserved for those who follow Jesus, or the clay pot, that will be smashed by the judgment of Christ for all who deny Him?

We too need to remember not to be so short-sighted in our lives. We often make the mistake of thinking that a little compromise in our lives will make our path a little smoother — and it may, but at what cost? A life of comfort, distraction, and indulgence here in this life is *not* worth being smashed like a clay pot in the next!

The final promise that Jesus makes to "him who overcomes" is in verse 28, "I will also give him the morning star." The morning star is the last star that appears just before dawn, when the night is coldest and darkest.

When our life seems to be at its coldest, darkest and bleakest, our faith in Jesus Christ as the coming King brings us hope. Do you remember the reaction of the Magi, shepherds, Simeon and Anna when they finally saw the long-awaited Messiah? They lived for a long time looking at the morning star, awaiting the dawn.

We too are looking at the morning star and awaiting the dawn of Christ's return. Remember that though it looks dark around us, morning is coming when Jesus will appear again and will shine His light on this world. He will come to expose evil and reward the faithful. He will rule with truth and perfect judgment. The morning star is the symbol of hope given to believers so that they can "hold on until he comes," or until "the end." Christ's victory will be theirs one day.

If The Shoe Fits

What more can really be said other than, "He who has an ear, let him hear what the Spirit says to the churches." Where are you in your sin life right now? I can guarantee this ... you *are* sinning. Believe it. The question is what are you doing about it? Are you willing to have Jesus delve deeper and deeper into the dark corners and closed closets of your heart and have Him sweep clean the dirty edges of your soul?

What areas of compromise are in your life? Have you compromised your doctrine, your faith, or the practice of your relationship with Jesus? Perhaps you haven't made it all the way through the five steps of repentance, and need to start making things right.

Are you looking for hope today? Find your hope in the Morning Star. Seek Him with all your heart and you will not be disappointed when the dawn comes.

CHAPTER SEVEN

Sardis: Reputation and Reality

Are you a camper? Do you love to look up at the night sky and see the stars twinkling into infinity, getting lost in the huge black expanse dotted with shimmering specks of fire? (Poetic, no?) I used to do it all the time. I haven't in a long while, but I used to love gazing up into the sky, especially when camping or driving outside of the city (whilst veering into oncoming traffic).

However, the great preacher, party-pooper John MacArthur reminded me of something during my study of this church. He asked the question, "Did you know that some of the stars that you are looking at may have gone out years ago?" Sadly, it's true.

Many stars are so far away that the light from them takes years just to reach earth. So if one explodes, or dies, we could be seeing its light for years without realizing that we are wishing upon a non-existent star. I googled "dying star" and found a great picture of a "light echo" from a star called Cassiopeia A which died in a supernova explosion about 325 years ago. The light of the star in the picture was still visible at least 50 years ago.

A star that looks alive to our eyes, but died a long time ago. The light is not a current reality, but light that was from the past. The reputation of the star remains, but the reality is that the light was extinguished long ago.

That's actually the story of the church that we are going to read about in this chapter. At one time, it was a bright and shining star of a church, full of people who served and worshipped the Lord, but that light had gone out. The reputation of the church remained, and those around them still saw light ... but when Jesus looked at the reality of the situation, all He saw was a dead star.

So again, and this should come as no surprise, go get your Bible and open it up and read Revelation 3:1-6. I'll wait here... Wait, can I use your bathroom?

The Address

Done? Super. Jesus addresses his fifth letter to the church in the city of Sardis.

The history of Sardis, in many ways, mirrors the history of the church within it. Sardis, 30 miles south of Thyatira, was founded in 1200 BC, and became one of the greatest cities in the ancient world.

It was the capital of the staggeringly wealthy Lydian kingdom. It was located at the intersection of five major highways, and was widely known for its riches and extravagance. Its wealth came from the gold found in the nearby Pactolus River, still famous today for the gold dust that can be found in it. In fact, they had so much gold that Sardis was the first city to ever mint gold and silver coins. Archaeologists have found hundreds of crucibles, furnaces used to refine precious metals. Even the dead were wealthy in Sardis as it boasted a large necropolis, a cemetery, with many ornate and beautiful burial mounds.

Aesop, the one who told many famous fables, is thought to have been from Sardis. The city also prided itself on being a major manufacturing centre. They not only invented coin minting, but claimed to have been the city that discovered how to dye wool.

But what made Sardis most unique was where it was located. Many cities were built on hills, even on the sides of mountains … but none could claim the kind of security that they had in Sardis. Sardis was built on one of the spurs that jutted out of the Tmolus Mountains, and stood 1500 feet from the valley below. It was considered to be almost impregnable. In fact, even in John's day there was a saying, "To capture the acropolis of Sardis," which meant the same thing as "doing the impossible." We would equate it to something like "Fort Knox" today. It was the embodiment of security and impenetrability.

Photo courtesy of Rex Geissler www.greatcommission.com

Three sides of the city were smooth perpendicular rock that, it was said, a child could defend. The only approach was from the south, via a steep, difficult path that was easily guarded by a very few soldiers (and you thought your gated community was safe).

The only problem was that there was a limited amount of room to expand the city, so they started a second city below. When a threat came, the people of the second city would flee up the pass to old Sardis for protection.

But, as I said, the story of the city, and the story of the church Jesus writes to are very similar. Though Sardis had a glorious past, the wealth and security led to overconfidence, and eventually led to the city's downfall.

In 549 BC Sardis was ruled by Croesus, King of Lydia. He wasn't content with his own kingdom and wanted to conquer even more lands. So he consulted the famous Oracle of Delphi and asked if it would be wise to wage war against King Cyrus of Persia. The Oracle, in the cryptic way that oracles do, said this, "If you cross the river to attack, a great nation will fall." It never occurred to Croesus that the nation would be his own.[vi]

In the year 546 BC he crossed the river and was soundly beaten by the Persians. He retreated to Sardis where he would be safe, and where he could rebuild his army. The Persians followed and laid siege to Sardis for two weeks, but couldn't gain entrance, and were getting frustrated. King Cyrus said that he would pay a large reward for anyone who could come up with a plan to breach the great keep of Sardis. Croesus felt so secure in his city, and so sure that the Persians would be easy pickings among the rocks and crags on his mountain, that by the end of the two weeks he was going to sleep without even stationing guards on all four walls. The only place he felt it necessary was the front gate.

Unbeknownst to him, earlier that day, while his own soldiers were walking along part of the wall, one of the men dropped his helmet down the side. Apparently he was some kind of a climber because he used a large fissure in the rock wall to shimmy down, retrieve his helmet and climb back up. All the while, one of the Persian soldiers was watching.

That night, the watchful soldier led a small band of Persians up the same fissure and over the unguarded wall. He found everyone in the city sound asleep, including the king and most of the soldiers. The only ones awake were a small group by the front gate. The Persians snuck their way to the main gate, beat the soldiers, and threw open the entrance so the rest of the Persian army could flood in and wreak havoc on sleeping Sardis.

Great story, and believe it or not, the same thing happened 350 years later in 218 BC when Antiochus the Great conquered Sardis scaling the same wall the same way.

Sardis became a Roman city in 133 BC, and was still wealthy and prosperous until a great earthquake came and destroyed it in 17 AD. The Emperor Tiberius sent much aid to rebuild, but it was never quite the same.

In John's day the city was a shadow of its former self, but still managed to look pretty good. There were half-built buildings everywhere giving the illusion of progress and wealth, but in truth, the city's glory days were long past. The city became a seedbed of moral decadence and decline; the people were lethargic, not building or working, resting on the laurels of their old reputation, and were mostly useless.

Description of Jesus

It is to the church in this city that Jesus writes His description, "These are the words of him who holds the seven spirits of God and the seven stars." This description of Jesus is meant to take the reader back to John's picture of Christ in the first chapter.

The "seven spirits" are another name for the Holy Spirit, the third member of the Trinity. Seven is the number of perfection. The "seven stars" are the seven pastors of the seven churches. Jesus reminds the group that life itself is held in His hand. He holds, and is, the Spirit of God, the source of all life … the breath of life.

The word "Spirit" is the same word as "breath" or "wind," the word PNEUMA. Genesis 2:7, the very beginning of human life, says, "The LORD God formed the man from the dust of the ground and breathed into his nostrils the breath of life, and the man became a living being" (Genesis 2:7). To the church Jesus is about to pronounce dead, He reminds them that He is the one who has the "breath of life." He invented life and death, and could grant it to anyone.

The "I Know" Statement

At this point the words to the church of Sardis start to get exceedingly stern. Jesus says, "I know your deeds; you have a reputation of being alive, but you are dead."

This is the first time that the letters contain no commendation or encouragement for a church. There is simply nothing good to report. There doesn't seem to be trouble with persecution or heresy, so no one is called "faithful." But then why would there be? Satan doesn't need to bother a church that's already dead.

Jesus' main concern, obviously, is the lack of life in the church, and the group of unregenerate, non-believers, non-Christians, that seems to be running the place and playing church. Remember, Jesus isn't talking to the city of Sardis, He's talking to the church within it. He says, "you have a reputation for being alive, but you are really dead."

Jesus seems to be drawing an analogy from the history and current events of the city at this point. Sardis had the reputation of being a lively city, but they were actually defeated, and declining. Outwardly they were fooling everybody, even themselves, but the truth was that they were always on the cusp of total defeat.

Jesus effectively says to this church, "You look to others like you are alive. You have the reputation of being a church. People who don't look too closely all assume that you're alive and doing my will. But you're not." Jesus said this same thing before, during His earthly ministry. If you remember, he was condemning the Jewish leaders in Matthew 23:27-28 and said, "Woe to you, teachers of the law and Pharisees, you hypocrites! You are like whitewashed tombs, which look beautiful on the outside but on the inside are full of dead men's bones and everything unclean. In the same way, on the outside you appear to people as righteous but on the inside you are full of hypocrisy and wickedness."

He said to these Pharisees, and to this church, "You look like a well-kept mausoleum. You're like a beautifully carved burial vault." Jesus equates the church and the people within it to a place like the Taj Mahal.

As large, beautiful and amazing as the building is ... it's just a house for dead bones. Jesus looks at this church in Sardis and tells them that they are not really a part of His kingdom. They are not really a live, growing, healthy church, but are a dead, rotting corpse with beautiful coverings. Like when we put make-up on, and dress dead bodies for funerals ... they have the illusion of life, but the reality is that the breath of life, the Spirit is gone, the PNEUMA is gone. What do we always say, "He looks like he is alive, but sleeping." But there are no vital signs, no beeps on the machines, no ability to work, or serve, or love, or teach; just a dead body, taking up space, with the illusion of life.

These people were Christian in name only; *nominal* Christians. They were not redeemed, they were not disciples of Jesus, they were not people who read and lived the words of the Bible, and they were not people who worshiped Jesus. They were not in a growing relationship with Jesus, but were just going through the motions of "doing church."

The Diagnosis

Gandhi once said, "I like your Jesus. I do not like your Christians. They are so unlike your Jesus." Jesus' first diagnosis for this church was that their *reputation* didn't match their *reality*.

I want to park here for a bit because I was really challenged by this; that my reputation needs to match my reality. Is what people think of me ... or what I think of myself ... the way that God sees me in truth? This church looked alive, but was really dead. Some people look like a Christian, sound like a Christian, even use all the Christianese words ... but are as far from being disciples of Jesus as they could be.

I was thinking about how far this really extended, and started to wander even farther down the trail with the concept. I hope you can follow along.

- Some people have the reputation of being a good athlete, but the reality is that they are full of performance-enhancing drugs, and are cheaters.
- Some have the reputation of being a good father, but inside, the reality is that they are putting themselves first and resent their children and families.

- Some have the reputation of being a good mother, but in reality, their kids don't respect them, love them or honour them, the truth is that they are afraid of them.
- Some have the reputation of being all put together, no fear, no worries, but in reality, they are holding on by a thread, and are terrified.

Churches can die, and people, like spiritual zombies, can feign spiritual life. What are some signs that a church is dead? Or that a Christian is really dead, though he or she pretends to be alive as a disciple of Jesus? I put together a list from various sources, and out of my own experience.

A Christian or Church is dead when...

...we are more concerned with how to DO worship, than how to BE a worshipper.

...we are more worried about social causes and special interests than telling the good news of Jesus Christ to lost people.

...we are more consumed by material things than spiritual ones.

...we are more worried about what other people say than what Jesus says.

...there is more talk about systems of theology and Bible trivia than the Word of God.

...gossip becomes more common than prayer.

...what happened on a TV show is shared more than what is happening in reality.

...we polish and fix the building, but neglect encouraging and helping the people.

...we are easy on ourselves, but tough on others.

...worship becomes a dead habit instead of communion with God.

...music is something to fight over, not sing together.

...people are afraid to be seen by others in the church because they are ashamed that the way they look will make them an object of gossip or scorn.

...we go home from service more drained than when we came.

...we glory in past successes, rather than striving for new ones.

Some people in this church will argue saying, "Look, we're doing something!" The church in Sardis would no doubt argue the point and say, "C'mon, we're doing things! We're active, we're ministering! We're working!" And Jesus gives His next diagnosis at the end of verse 2, "I have not found your deeds *complete* in the sight of my God."

Just like the half-built buildings that were scattered around the city of Sardis, many that we can still see today, the church of Sardis' deeds were incomplete. There was motion, even busy-ness, but in God's eyes, it was incomplete. Why? Because it lacked two things.

First, the acts weren't being governed by Him. This dead church wasn't praying and asking for God's will, and was therefore doing a lot of things that were unnecessary, and even harmful as a result. If you've ever seen the movie "Weekend at Bernie's," you know what I'm talking about. We can go through the motions of propping up our dead spirituality, tie strings to it, run programs, dress it up, and seem like we're doing ministry, but all along we are only lying to ourselves and even damaging ourselves and our community.

Second, and just as important if not more so, this church wasn't doing whatever they were doing with love. Ephesians 4:16 tells us that the body of Christ is fed and built up by the love Jesus has for us, by the love shared between members of the church, and by their love for those who are unsaved. The church wasn't worshipping God in their actions, nor was it acting out of love, and so the body wasn't fed ... and so it died. They were spiritual zombies, only consuming church, and were living a lie.

The saddest part of the whole thing was that they didn't even know it. They were once strong and vibrant, but were now dead. It reminds us of the story from the Old Testament, the story of Samson.

Most of us know the story; the man who seemed to be like everyone else, but had a supernatural strength which God gave him to conquer the Philistines. He falls in love with one of the enemy, a Philistine woman named Delilah who pesters and nags him into revealing the secret of his strength so he can be taken captive by her kin. He eventually tells her that if his hair were cut then he'd be as weak as everyone else.

But it wasn't about the hair ("Darned tootin'!", say the baldies). The hair didn't give him strength ... the Spirit of God did. Throughout the story of Samson we see how, even though God was faithful, Samson continued to make selfish choices and drive God further and further from Him.

The story ends like this in Judges 16, "When Delilah saw that he had told her everything, she sent word to the rulers of the Philistines, 'Come back once more; he has told me everything.' So the rulers of the Philistines returned with the silver in their hands. Having put him to sleep on her lap, she called a man to shave off the seven braids of his hair, and so began to subdue him. And his strength left him. Then she called, 'Samson, the Philistines are upon you!' He awoke from his sleep and thought, 'I'll go out as before and shake myself free.' *But he did not know that the LORD had left him.* Then the Philistines seized him, gouged out his eyes and took him down to Gaza. Binding him with bronze shackles, they set him to grinding in the prison."

The church of Sardis, like Samson, was getting up and going through the motions, not even realizing that the Lord had left them.

It's been said that churches today have too many members that are merely Christians in proclamation only. They want to be known for helping the poor, supporting evangelism, being good worshippers, and faithful Christians ... but they are nowhere to be found when the work is to be done. On the other end of things, there are people who do a lot in the church, but are doing it just so that they can be seen by others -- not to serve others in the name of Jesus, but for the strokes that come with being known in the church. They keep up the appearances of being a dedicated Christian, but they lack the love, the heart of worship, the humility, and the joy of service that Jesus expects. In short, they are "hypocrites" (from the Greek word HYPROKITES meaning "play actors").

The Prescription

To this Church Jesus says, "WAKE UP!" Wake up and realize that they are dead. Then he gives two prescriptions of what to do after they "wake up." First, "Strengthen what remains and is about to die!" What does that mean?

Take a look at verse 4 and we get a clue. "Yet you have a few people in Sardis who have not soiled their clothes." There is a little remnant group of Christians who are still alive. Jesus encourages them to take a look at the remnant of people that the church has been treating so poorly, and start to learn how to live by watching them. Jesus is saying, "But don't just watch them, make the effort to strengthen them. Listen to them, and do what they do. Go to the meetings they go to, pray for what they are praying for, serve in the ministries that they are serving in. Find out their heart, and mimic it, because they are mimicking me! Strengthen them. Give them the resources to grow the little ministry that they have there! Join them, or get out of the way. Fan the flames of the dying embers of the spirituality that is still left in your church."

God, in His mercy, always seems to leave a remnant of good people to show the right way to live and serve Him. Sardis had one, and I would say that many dead churches today do as well. Jesus says, "Get a hold of those people, listen to them, support them, live like them, and help them in any way you can. Strengthen what remains."

Jesus' second prescription, in verse 3, we've heard before, "Remember, therefore, what you have received and heard; obey it, and repent." Do you remember? The same as Ephesus: Remember, repent and do. In this case it's, "remember, obey and repent."

"Remember" your relationship with Jesus, and your commitment to Him. Get back to reading and hearing the word of God, talking to Jesus and building that relationship with Him. "Repent" from the wrong things you've done, or haven't done right. And "obey," or "do" the things that you are supposed to be doing.

Sometimes it's so simple it's scary. Get back to the apostolic teaching about Jesus as the central focus of your ministry, repent from sin, and start acting like Christians. And if you can't remember how to act like Christians ... then take a look at that little remnant group and get a good reminder.

"If You Don't"

Jesus says, "But if you do not wake up, I will come like a thief, and you will not know at what time I will come to you." Jesus seems to be again referring to the conquering of Sardis. Just like that little group of soldiers who crawled up that fissure and surprised the whole city, Jesus too will come like a thief and surprise the church.

This most likely isn't a reference to the second coming of Jesus, but is more likely a threat, or rather a promise, of imminent judgment. If this church doesn't "repent" and "strengthen what remains," then Jesus is going to come and wipe it off the map. The dead church would be removed because dead things carry diseases that affect living beings. Their name would be erased, and the little remnant of believers scattered. No more church in Sardis.

"Wake up!" Jesus says. See that Jesus is coming. Be aware that He takes His church, which He loves very much, most seriously ... and either "wake up" or succumb to judgment.

"If You Do"

The only way we can welcome this "holy surprise" and not be worried about His arrival, is if we are walking securely in a daily relationship with

Him. Who worries about someone that they know personally, trust dearly, and walk with daily?

Jesus says in verse 5, "He who overcomes will, like them, be dressed in white. I will never blot out his name from the book of life, but will acknowledge his name before my Father and his angels."

For those that do "repent," "strengthen what remains" and have not "soiled their clothes", Jesus has 3 promises.

First, they will be dressed in White. Primarily the meaning of these white clothes is to represent purity and holiness, the forgiveness of God that will be shown in gleaming white. Jesus was seen wearing white during the transfiguration. God's holy angels are often seen wearing white in scripture. The elders and the martyrs for the faith are all wearing white clothes in Revelation. It is the dress colour of the holiness and perfection of heaven.

But there are other meanings as well. For example, those who were victorious in battle were often clothed in white and heralded for their great deeds. People still wear white in their weddings to celebrate the special occasion. The church, very early on, started dressing their baptismal candidates in white to representing the perfect forgiveness and the washing away of their sins. Jesus' first promise is that He will dress the faithful in white.

Second, Jesus says, "I will never blot his name out of the book of life." Grumpy people tend to turn this promise into a threat, saying that this means that some people will be blotted out of the book. But this is a freedom text, not a warning text. This verse has *nothing to do with blotting people out* ... that's not even in there! It has everything to do with Jesus promise that He will NEVER blot their names out of the "book of life," the heavenly roster of people that are saved.

In ancient days names were written into city registers to show who the citizens were. Special citizens would have their names inscribed with gold letters. When a citizen died, or was convicted of a capital crime, his or her name would be erased from the city book and they would lose their citizenship.

Jesus promises that He will never be like the city officials who would erase people from citizenship books. He will never blot their name out of the book! Revelation 13:8 tells us that the "book of life" has one owner, the "Lamb of God," Jesus Christ. Those written in this book are in there because of the gift of salvation given by God, and their status there is based on the sufficiency of the sacrifice of Jesus for their sins. His blood covers all sin, and is the security by which we can know our salvation is assured. Romans 8 says that there is "no condemnation for those who are in Jesus Christ" because we have been set free by Him. It also says that we are joint heirs to the promises of Jesus, and are sons and daughters of God. Our Good Father never turns His back on His children.

Third, Jesus promises He "will acknowledge his name before my Father and his angels." Jesus promises that He will proclaim and testify on behalf of all those who put faith in Him and live lives worthy of that relationship.

In pagan religions it was forbidden to approach a god with dirty clothes. A person had to be clean in order to come into the temple. Jesus demolishes that concept. He invites soiled, sinful, dirty people to come into His presence, so that *He can clean them*, and give them new clothes, so they may be presented to the Father.

Romans 8 continues with one of the greatest promises ever written. Paul tells us, "If God is for us, who can be against us? ... Who will bring any charge against those whom God has chosen? It is God who justifies. Who is he that condemns? Christ Jesus, who died—more than that, who was raised to life—is at the right hand of God and is also interceding for us. Who shall separate us from the love of Christ? ... Shall trouble or hardship or persecution or famine or nakedness or danger or sword? ... For I am convinced that neither death nor life, neither angels nor demons, neither the present nor the future, nor any powers, neither height nor depth, nor anything else in all creation, will be able to separate us from the love of God that is in Christ Jesus our Lord."

If The Shoe Fits

Jesus ends every letter saying, "He who has an ear, let him hear what the Spirit says to the churches." The zombies that were playing church in Sardis needed to heed Jesus' warning of impending judgment. Indifferent believers needed to "wake up" before it was too late to save the church. Only a few could take comfort that they were written in the lamb's book of life and didn't need to worry about the surprise that would be coming when they least expected it.

Some good news is that Sardis seems to have actually headed Jesus' warnings to "repent" and "strengthen what remains." We know that there was a church there over 100 years later by a piece of a passionate Easter sermon given by a preacher named Melito.

Jesus desires that the individuals in His church "repent" and "strengthen what remains." What is God asking you to repent from, or what good things are you doing that need to be strengthened?

Jesus holds the "seven spirits," the Holy Spirit, and will gladly impart the "Breath of Life" to any who calls on His name … do you need new life today?

Jesus also holds "the seven stars," the ministers, and will gladly give earthly help to those who ask. Are you prepared to ask for help to "wake up" and reconnect with Jesus?

CHAPTER EIGHT

Philadelphia: The Open Door

There are not many places that you are going to find in North American culture these days where it is a good thing to be called "ordinary." Everyone wants to be unique, grab their 15 minutes of fame, and ride it out for as long as they can.

According to their webpage, Professor Jean Twenge of San Diego State University, in a study of 16,000 college students across the United States between1982 and 2006, found that students are far more narcissistic than they've ever been before. She created a Narcissistic Personality Inventory and gave it to the students to fill out (of course, all the people who thought they'd "probably just fail the test anyway" never took it ... ba-dum-ching!), with some surprising results.

The test asked people to rate themselves on various statements like, "If I ruled the world, it would be a better place." "I think I am a special person." "I can live my life any way I want to." "I like to be the centre of attention." It turns out that if you give people a test that asks them if they think they're better than everyone else, that they'll say "Yes!"

We may, in our less lucid moments, think that our students today are far more globally minded, are good recyclers, think about others, and are ready to help when needed. After all, they've lived through 8 billion after-school specials and Public Service Announcements, haven't they?

Well, according to Professor Twenge, "Far from being civically oriented, young people born after 1982 are the most narcissistic generation in recent history."

Of course, being born in 1978, I'm much more humble, grounded and civically oriented than my younger brother. In fact, I'm the most humble person I know. Actually, now that I think about it, on a scale of 1 to 10 ... I'm like a 12 on the humble scale. So there.

I can imagine why people all think that they are "special." There are no "x"s on tests anymore, only the right answers get a check mark. There is no more losing at sports anymore, because we don't keep score. At the end of the year, EVERYONE gets a trophy! We have people who are "famous for being famous." Canadian Idol, America's Got Talent, and every rags-to-riches story we are told in the newspaper have us convinced that everyone in society is just shy of their big break. It's a strange world in which nobody is ordinary, and everybody is "special."

I hate to burst your bubble, but you might just be ordinary. Heck... I just might be ordinary! The job you do may be an ordinary job. The family you grew up in may be an ordinary family. The church you attend may be an ordinary church.

The church in Philadelphia is just an ordinary church. Joe Community Church of Philadelphia. It's not Ephesus, the church that started it all. It's not Sardis, the super-rich church. It's not even Smyrna, targeted by Satan and under attack. It's just Joe Church.

The story of this church is not the story of this church ... it's the story of what Jesus is going to do with this ordinary, regular, everyday, little church.

You know by now that this is the point in which you need to open up your Bible and read Revelation 3:7-13, right? I'll wait here ... flexing my enormous muscles.

The Address

Done? Good.

Not much is known about the little city of Philadelphia in the ancient Roman province of Asia in Asia Minor, 28 miles southeast of Sardis.

It was founded by King Eumenes in the middle of the second century, who named it as a testament to the love he had for his brother Attalus II, who would be his successor to the throne. Hence the name of the city, Philadelphia, PHILIA meaning "affectionate love," and DELPHOS meaning "brother."

King Attalus II's successor was his nephew Attalus III who took over kingship of the region in 138 BC, but died only a few years later without an heir and bequeathed the region and city to his Roman allies in 133 BC.

There are a couple of important things that we do know about the city, and they help us understand Jesus' letter to them better.

First, this community was a gateway city. It was planted by King Eumenes, and was utilized later by the Romans for a very specific purpose. It was to be the gateway to the entire province, and was placed right on the road which was the best way to ascend from the valley to the higher plateau where most of the rest of the province sat. People would travel via the valley, and when they wanted to enter the area, they would take a certain path to get up the 2500 feet from the Hermus Valley to the vast central plateau.

This was a great place to put Philadelphia, because it made the city a natural doorway to the rest of the area. Of course it was a physical doorway: you had to go through the city to get to the rest of the province. It was also the doorway of communication: Rome's Imperial Postal service, the national mail service, went through Philadelphia. It was a doorway of commerce: the great volcanic region around it made it great for vineyards, and Philadelphia was a major source of wine.

It was also a doorway of culture: Greek culture permeated Philadelphia, and it was the city's unwritten task to Hellenize the rest of the people in the area. In fact, they were so successful in spreading their culture and language that by 19 AD the Lydian language, which was the primary tongue of the region, was almost entirely replaced by Greek.

The second most important thing we need to know about Philadelphia was that it was a shaky city. The giant earthquake of 17 AD that we looked at during the study of Sardis, also rocked Philadelphia, and in fact destroyed the city. But while Sardis was rebuilding with the great wealth sent from Emperor Tiberius, Philadelphia could hardly build anything. The city was founded on a fault line, and felt aftershocks constantly for more than twenty years. The Greek historian Strabo who lived during this time wrote: "Philadelphia has no trustworthy walls, but daily in one direction or another they keep tottering and falling apart."

Consequently, people would come into the city during the day to do business, but would then leave in the evenings to homes and huts built outside the city. To live and build inside Philadelphia was considered to be foolishness because there was no way to be sure how long the house you lived in would stand! That stigma would have persisted even into the time of the writing of Jesus' letter. People used many different methods and techniques to try to keep their homes together during the quakes and tremors, but the people were always in fear of the next big one that would decimate the city.

The Description of Jesus

It is to this city that Jesus describes Himself in verse 7 saying, "These are the words of him who is holy and true, who holds the key of David. What he opens no one can shut, and what he shuts no one can open." This is really a threefold description, and is unique in that it is not a direct quote from the first chapter, like all the other descriptions Christ uses for Himself.

First, Jesus says this letter is from "him who is holy and true." An alternate translation of this would be to say "the Holy One." This is a title for God. Jesus says, "I'm God." This phrase is used throughout the Old and New Testaments as a title for God.

In 2 Kings 19:22 God is called, "The Holy One of Israel." In Isaiah 43:15 God says of Himself, "I am the LORD, your Holy One, Israel's Creator, your King." In the New Testament, when Mary is first told that she is going to have a baby named Jesus, she is told, "The Holy Spirit will come upon you, and the power of the Most High will overshadow you. So *the holy one* to be born will be called the Son of God" (Luke 1:35). And in Mark 1, just before Jesus casts a demon out of a man, it cried out, "What do you want with us, Jesus of Nazareth? Have you come to destroy us? I know who you are—the Holy One of God!"

These two words used to describe God are very important to our understanding of who God and Jesus are. First, He is "holy." That means He is different, separate, special, perfect and pure. When God gives us the promise that when we accept Him as our saviour, that He will make us "Holy" He means, "I will make you separate and special from the rest of the world, and purify you from all sin, making you different from everyone outside My Kingdom." God is the ultimate holiness.

If you want to get a picture of holiness, sanctification, or separateness, you don't have to look any farther than grandma's china cabinet, or your own hockey-card collection. When you collect this stuff, what do you do? You make it holy, or "set-apart." You put the cards in special sleeves or the baseball on a high shelf. Everything that is even remotely special in our house, because we have kids, is at least 5 feet off the ground; we have "made it holy, separate and special."

When we sing to God that He is "Holy, Holy, Holy," that's what we are saying. That He is exceptional, set apart, high, unique, and holds a special place in our hearts and lives. The great thing is that God says that to us!

The second of Jesus' descriptions of Himself says that He is "One," or our translation here, "True." The word there means real, authentic, and complete. The declaration of Moses to the people of Israel before he gave the Law was this, "Hear, O Israel: The LORD our God, the LORD is one" (Deut 6:4). He is complete and not lacking in anything, and is completely authentic in all He does. There is no deception in Him. We can trust Him, and nothing can change that. That is very encouraging for those of us who feel the tumult in the lives we live right now. It's encouraging to know that when God says something, when He makes a promise, that we can take it to the bank. With all the changes and confusion in the world today, what else in this world can give us that kind of comfort, peace and assurance?

The third description Jesus gives in this letter to Philadelphia is that He "holds the Key of David." The simple meaning of this is that keys symbolize control. Jesus says here, "I'm the Key Man." Jesus has control and authority over the entrance to the throne room and presence of the King, God.

In ancient days, the key holder was second in authority only to the King. If you want to read something really neat, open up and read Isaiah 22:15-25. This is the Old Testament passage that Jesus is asking the readers to remember.

It is the passing of the keys of the kingdom of Israel from Shebna to Eliakim. Shebna was a non-Jewish, Egyptian, a foreigner who had risen in power to become the key holder to the king. But he became prideful and arrogant and wanted to be honoured and buried like the King, so he started to carve his own ornate burial plot ... something that was a smack in the face to the king and the kingdom. So he was removed and a better, truer, more worthy key holder was chosen. That's the picture Jesus gives here. He's a better, truer, more trustworthy, key holder to the presence of God, who is willing and able to grant access to the King and Kingdom of Heaven to all who go through Him.

Fourth, Jesus says, "What he opens no one can shut, and what he shuts no one can open." Jesus says, "I am God." He says, "I'm the Key Man." And then he says, "I am the Doorman." This is a declaration of Jesus' omnipotence as God. I've already mentioned the blazing eyes of Jesus, or the *omniscience* of Jesus, but here we see His declaration of His absolute power, His *omnipotence.*

When Jesus mentions doors here, He brings up another Isaiah passage (Isn't it amazing that when Jesus speaks, He speaks with such amazing depth and care, always tying in things He's said before so we can always learn more about Him?). In Isaiah 43:13 God says, "When I act, who can reverse it?" When Jesus, the doorman, opens a door, or closes one, there's no one who can change it. Whether it's the doorway to salvation, and the open invitation to heaven, or a doorway of opportunity in our lives, if God opens it, it stays open, and if He closes it, it says closed.

I find this very encouraging as I'm sure the Philadelphia church did as well. When God wants something to happen, it happens, and there is no way that anybody else is going to mess it up. This struggling, persecuted, ordinary church in Philadelphia on shaky ground because of all the earthquakes and because its people were under attack for their faith, needed hope. Jesus knew that they would find great hope and cheer in the fact that when it looks like things are grim, and that nothing's really shaking in their lives, He loves them, and He is the one who controls the doors of opportunity.

Missionaries know about this. Sometimes what looks like a great loss becomes a great gain. It seems, based on some articles I've read in the newspapers, that China is beginning to kick all of the evangelical missionaries out of their country—again. Now, while this looks pretty devastating, as though the ministry there is on its last legs, we've seen this before.

In 1865 a man from England by the name of J. Hudson Taylor decided to dedicate his life to the service of the gospel in mainland China. He never asked anyone for financial help and he even began to dress like the Chinese people, something that was not done among missionaries of his time. He formed the China Inland Mission and recruited other students from England to help him reach the Chinese. By

1949, when China started kicking them out, CIM had sent over 6,000 missionaries into China's interior.

There was nothing that was going to shut the door of the gospel there. It is now, even under an oppressive communist government, one of the fastest growing evangelical movements in the world.

Here's the truth for us today: if God has been knocking in your heart, and has been opening the door before you to change your life, there is nothing that anyone can do to shut it. If there is an opportunity that He wants to give you, or a gift that He wants to make available to you, there is nothing that will close that door. Now, He won't walk through the door for you. He's not going to pick you up and toss you through the door … but He will open it for you.

Also, when God closes a door, no one can open it. Sometimes we try to slam our way through things, and we end up messing it up. We try to crash through a door that God has closed and we end up only hurting ourselves. We force ourselves into a situation that *we* want, and that we think would be best for us, and 20/20 hindsight shows us that we shouldn't have pushed our way in there. We just ended up harming ourselves and others.

Sometimes the door He opens is only open for a time. He asks for our obedience in that moment, and if we are not listening, or are being disobedient, we miss the opportunity and the door closes. Like in the other letters where Jesus says, "if you repent and overcome, then you will receive blessing, but if you choose to keep sinning, then you will receive judgment." It's a time thing. You only have a certain amount of time, and once the door is closed, no one can re-open it.

A quick example out of my life is when I tell my kids that they have a certain amount of time to clean their room, and if they do it in that amount of time, then we can go have a treat. If they take too long, if they don't clean their room, if they choose to mess around … then the door of opportunity, *that I want to give them*, passes them by, and it closes for the day.

The "I Know" Statement & The Diagnosis

Jesus says, "I know your deeds." Again, this means, "I have intimate knowledge of what is going on in your life and church." And this allows Him to make His diagnosis. And there are 3 parts to the diagnosis of this church.

We skip a sentence and see what Jesus diagnoses first, "I know you have little strength." At first glance this may seem like an accusation; like

Jesus is saying, "you are weak." But it's not an indictment, it's a compliment. He says, "I know you have little strength, yet you have kept my word and have not denied my name."

This small, shaky little church was, no doubt, wondering if Jesus had all but abandoned them, since they were so few in numbers, nothing "special" was happening, and they were so tired. Many of them were poor, possibly homeless, and were tired of the persecution and the difficulty of being a disciple of Jesus. But they had "kept his word" even though they were weak, meaning they had lived the way the Bible says to live, and the way the apostles had taught them to. They had proved that they loved Jesus, and served Him as Lord, by obeying His commands.

And they had also, "not denied His name," meaning that they had faced the daily pressures from the trade guilds, the government and the people in the city, and the scornful Jews, and they had not denied Jesus and sacrificed to the Emperor or the many idols, but had stayed true to Him.

Jesus commends this little church for their faithfulness. In verse 10 Jesus commends them further by saying that they had "kept his command to endure patiently." This is a more sweeping encouragement, meaning that they had taken Jesus seriously when He had said that because of Him they would face many problems.

In Matthew 10:22 Jesus said, "All men will hate you because of me, but he who stands firm [*who endures*] to the end will be saved." The church was under some tough times, was under persecution, and was constantly under temptation, but the little strength they had left was committed to building up and sustaining their relationship with Jesus. Consequently, they were enduring their persecution well, were living the way the Apostles taught them, and were still meeting together and serving each other.

Often when the hard times begin to roll, what do we do? Perhaps you do what I'm prone to doing. Maybe you tend to avoid church, rather than come to it. Avoid friends, prayer groups, family, etc. Stop talking to Jesus, stop reading the Bible. I figured God was mad at me, so I didn't want to talk to Him. Or that I'd somehow get back at Him by avoiding Him. That's not what the people of the church in Philadelphia did. They faced their problems and ordinariness by drawing closer to Jesus.

The Prescription

So Jesus gives them His prescription. And the prescription also, has 3 parts. And now we back up a bit to the beginning of verse 8.

First Jesus says, "I know your deeds. See, I have placed before you an open door that no one can shut." The Key Holder; the Doorman of Heaven, because of their faithfulness and strength, is telling them that He has opened a door for them. There has been a lot of ink spilled about this phrase. It could mean two things. As far as I'm concerned, I believe it means both.

The open door represents the doorway to salvation – the door that no one can shut. No one can take away the salvation that Jesus has bought with His blood. But the second meaning, I believe, is more likely. Jesus says, "I have placed *before you* an open door." This implies that they have not walked through it yet. He's talking to a church full of saved people, after all. I believe that this is the door for the opportunity to grow their church and spread the gospel. Jesus is going to give them the chance to strengthen their church, to gain members, and to share the gospel in a new, exciting and meaningful way that was going to impact their little, ordinary church in a big way.

Remember that Philadelphia was a gateway, or a doorway city, to the rest of the province. This not only made it a great place to put the mail carriers and to disseminate the Greek language; it also made it a great place for the Gospel to spread.

The great missionary Paul uses the same "open door" phrase multiple times during his ministry. In 1 Corinthians 16:8-9 Paul says, "But I will stay on at Ephesus until Pentecost, because a *great door for effective work* has opened to me." In 2 Corinthians 2:12 he says, "Now when I went to Troas to preach the gospel of Christ and found that the Lord had *opened a door* for me." In Colossians 4:2-3 Paul writes from prison, "Devote yourselves to prayer, being watchful and thankful. And pray for us, too, that God may *open a door* for our message, so that we may proclaim the mystery of Christ, for which I am in chains."

I believe that Jesus' gift to the church, this "door," is "open" because of their faithfulness during difficult times, and ordinary times, and because of their love for each other. His gift is to open up the door for church growth, for the gospel to be told, for people's lives to be affected by the grace of God, and most of all, for people to be saved. Ultimately, this is a major part of what God wants from us in the world. I'm sure that this is His favourite door to open. The door to affecting people's lives in such a way that they come to saving faith in Him, and turn from a life of sin and selfishness into amazing, effective kingdom followers.

But these two dynamics go hand in hand – faithfulness and open doors. We do our best, we live our lives His way, and He opens doors. When we are revelling in sin, sloth, greed, envy, anger, bitterness, or whatever else, God isn't going to be opening doors for us.

Sometimes I'm very foolish in my asking things of God. I ask God to increase the effectiveness of my ministry, to help me win more people to Him, to help my family to love each other more, to help me do better in my spending, to help me flee from sin. But I don't follow it up with obedience and faithful living.

Am I putting the work and the study time into becoming a better student of the Bible so I can be a more effective preacher and minister? Am I connecting with people in the church to learn about how to be a better pastor? Am I putting myself in situations during the week where I can meet new people and talk to them about Jesus? Am I being an example of love, humility and service to my family and my kids? Am I watching my money and avoiding unnecessary spending? Am I putting myself into situations where I know that I have a tendency to be tempted, or am I avoiding those places so that they are not as much of a problem?

How hypocritical is it of me to ask God to do anything, and then not be willing to follow it up with faithful service so He can do that work in me?

"God, please help me!" And God says, "I absolutely will … here's what to do." And I reply, "No God, I don't want to DO anything … just make it happen. Just make me thinner, smarter, more well read, a better evangelist, a better dad, a harder worker, better with my money…" And God says, "I *will*, but you *must be faithful to do what I ask* of you, and I will hone your character and finish the work." God opens doors for those who live faithfully for Him.

The second part of the prescription is in verse 9, "I will make those who are of the synagogue of Satan, who claim to be Jews though they are not, but are liars—I will make them come and fall down at your feet and acknowledge that I have loved you."

This is the bonus. A bonus like when you find out that you've been bumped up to first class seating on your flight. Or when you order a box of 10 chicken nuggets and you get 11. With this open door that Jesus places before them comes a bonus. All the people who said that they were wrong and unfaithful … will look like fools. All the people who said that it wasn't worth all that they were going through … all the people who told them that they were being far too fanatical in their faith … those who were accusing them of disobeying God … all the ones who told them that their current suffering, or "ordinariness" was a judgment on their faithfulness … they'd all be proven wrong.

Especially the Jews and Jewish converts in the area. Just like in Smyrna, the other church that Jesus commends, the Jewish people here were a problem. Some commentators I've read, and I'm apt to agree with them, say that instead of saying "the Jews," we today should read it as "the Baptists, the Lutherans, or another kind of Christian church." The idea here is that another group *of supposed believers* were their most difficult source of criticism and confrontation.

These Jews were supposed to be a people of God, but they were actually working for Satan. Jesus opens a door before this church, and all the other "believers" kept saying was that they were doing it wrong, worshipping wrong, acting wrong, and serving God wrong. It was very likely that they were accusing the Christians of being a "church of Satan." In fact, *they* were the group that was calling themselves a "church of God" but they were really working for Satan, because they were confronting, criticizing and actively persecuting God's people.

The words "fall down" in the original Greek actually means "to kiss the hand towards," which was a gesture of respect and reverence in ancient times. These detractors weren't going to worship the Christians, but respect them. As the church was faithful, and as they walked through the door Jesus opened, as they continued to deepen their relationship with Him, their critics would be absolutely embarrassed by the amount of blessing that they would see God pouring out on this little church, and would be forced to acknowledge they were wrong.

The third part of the prescription is really a promise, in verse 10, "Since you have kept my command to endure patiently, I will also keep you from the hour of trial that is going to come upon the whole world to test those who live on the earth."

Whew! Ok … don't get too excited. Some of you are looking at this verse and saying, "Oh, great, here we go." And others of you are absolutely salivating at the thought of an expositional study of this verse. Well, you're both going to be disappointed.

This is a great verse, and a lot of people have spent a lot of time talking about it, but I'm only going to give you the broad strokes.

Jesus' promise here extends beyond just the current happenings in Philadelphia. It extends beyond the church and the people that were reading this letter. We could call this, if you were reading a high-fallootin'-type book, *a revelatory promise for the future consummation of the coming messianic kingdom* (It's ok if you didn't understand that last sentence, I don't really either).

Basically, this verse is a reinforcement of what we've been saying all along: that these letters are not just written for a specific church at a specific time, but they transcend time, and speak to the church throughout the ages, and also to us here today.

This little sentence draws the reader into anticipation of reading the rest of the book of Revelation. What does Jesus mean by the "hour of trial that is going to come upon the whole world and test those who live on the earth?" He describes it in the rest of this book. The rest of the book spells out what the "hour of trial" or the "tribulation" is going to look like, and what it means for the faithful who live before, during, and after it.

Ok, I'll throw some of you a bone. This is a key verse for people who are pre-tribulation (Again, it's OK if you don't know what that means, it's not *that* important). For those who do know, this is the key verse that "pre-tribbers" point to in order to make their case that humanity will not be on earth during the seven-year tribulation, but will be raptured. Ok, now that all three of you are happy, let's continue.

There are different ways to take this verse, and it all hinges on the words, "keep you from," as in "I will *keep you from* the hour of trial." It either means that Christians *won't go through* the time of trial, the great tribulation described in Revelation. Or it means that God will *sustain them through* the great tribulation. Or it means that God will *sustain the church through the general trials* and tests and tribulations that will just come throughout regular life that everyone goes through.

I'm not going to commit much of this chapter to this, but it is a great promise. Whatever the end result of your personal view of this verse is, the fact that God takes care of His people is a great comfort to me. Do you see the theme here running throughout this whole letter to Philadelphia? God is in control. Jesus has the keys. Jesus opens and closes the doors of salvation and opportunities in this world. Jesus takes care of His people. Jesus strengthens His church.

The bottom line here is that when we look for strength within ourselves to tough our way though life's problems … we're always going to come up short. But when we put our faith in Jesus and in His strength … we'll always have far more than we need! Jesus is the key to enduring all the things we go through in this life, if we'd only be faithful in putting Him at the forefront of all we do!

If You Do

Notice, there is no "If you don't" statement to this church. Their faithfulness has already proved that they will continue to obey. So Jesus doesn't need to remind them of what will happen if they chose not to obey. He says, "I am coming soon." That's a great encouragement to us! When all else fails, and things look too tough ... that's the promise that has held the persecuted, frustrated, ordinary churches secure for centuries ... that Jesus is coming soon.

"Hold on to what you have, so that no one will take your crown." Another translation here is "hold fast to what you have, don't let anyone take your crown which is life." Meaning? Don't let anyone take away the joy and the hope that is our life in Christ and convince you to exist in a *dead faith*. No one can take our salvation, but they can try to convince us that it's boring and irrelevant. No one can close the door to heaven, but they can try to convince us that we don't need to talk to Jesus, that our faith doesn't impact our Monday to Saturday, and that as soon as we get baptized we need to walk around like we lost our best friend and look like we live on concentrated lemon juice! Somehow they will convince us that the only exciting things in life are outside of the church and a relationship with Jesus. Jesus implores the people to not let anyone take their "crown of life," their real Christian life, away from them and to exist in a dry, monotonous, uninteresting faith.

And to those who live a faithful life as though their relationship with Jesus matters, He makes three promises.

First, "Him who overcomes I will make a pillar in the temple of my God." The initial promise is a great one, especially for the Philadelphians. Pillars were usually the only thing left standing after one of the many earthquakes. They symbolized strength and security ... something that was severely lacking in the life of the Philadelphians, and in many of our lives today too. Things and people that can be counted on when life gets turbulent and all else is shaky are in short supply. But Jesus says that those who ground themselves in Him will be made strong and secure.

Matthew 16:16 is Peter's confession to Jesus that "You are the Christ, the Son of the living God." Jesus commends Peter saying, "on this rock I will build my church." Jesus Christ, the Son of the living God, is the solid bedrock of our faith, which the church is built on.

In 1 Timothy 3:15, the church is called the "pillar and foundation of truth." Check this out, because it's important: those that build their lives on *the solid bedrock* of "the Son of the living God," and participate in the church, "*the foundation* of truth," will be made into what Jesus calls strong and sturdy *pillars.*

What does that mean? He'll hone our character into being someone that can be counted on not to sway and falter when the earthquakes of life come. Someone who can be trusted. Someone whose whole existence is built on solid bedrock, a firm foundation, and won't sway when all else does.

He will turn us into people that, when the seismic activity and hurricane winds of life come … though everything around them falls and crashes … they are the ones left behind, standing firm. That's the kind of person Jesus wants us to be. It's the first promise to those who are faithful.

The second promise Jesus says, "Never again will he leave it." Not only will they be secure and strong, but they will always have a place in His home. The Philadelphians would flee the city every night to escape the tremors and the worry of the earthquakes. Jesus promises those who believe in Him that there is nowhere more secure than being with Him. Psalm 18:2 says, "The LORD is my rock, my fortress and my deliverer; my God is my rock, in whom I take refuge. He is my shield and the horn of my salvation, my stronghold." In this life where there is not much security, comfort or protection, there is a security and a home available for any who would come.

The third promise, and there are some here who will appreciate this more than others, is that Jesus will give the faithful believer a series of tattoos. (What did the Baptist preacher say?!? Jesus gives tattoos? Yes, yes he does.)

The first tattoo, "I will write on him the name of my God." What does it mean when we tattoo a name on us? (Anybody out there with a "Mother" on their arm?) It's someone we love, that we want to remember always, someone we want to honour, someone we've dedicated our life to, and someone who possesses our heart. Jesus' first tattoo, the name of God, reminds the believer who loves them and to whom they've committed their lives.

The second tattoo, "I will write on him … the name of the city of my God, the new Jerusalem, which is coming down out of heaven from my God." I've always wanted a tattoo of the Canadian flag on my ~~forehead~~ shoulder. I've seen lots of people with American flags, Canadian flags, Mexican flags, and even Greek and Irish flags. It designates where their home is, where their heart is, where they long to be, and where they feel safest.

Jesus' second tattoo reminds the believer where their true citizenship is, and where they will always call home. When the world seems alien and strange and people are not making the same decisions you are making because they seem to have a different playbook. When you look around and wonder why everyone is doing things so differently. When you feel like you stick out like a sore thumb, and can't get a grasp of what's going on around you … that tattoo reminds you that you are not home yet, but are a citizen of a different kingdom, built on different standards, with a different leader. You are a sojourner, but you will be home someday.

Jesus' third tattoo, "and I will also write on him my new name." Names in the Bible reveal character and destiny. When Jesus tattoos His new name on His people it means that He commits Himself to helping each person become who He designed them to be.

If The Shoe Fits

"He who has an ear, let him hear what the Spirit says to the churches." Is this the kind of relationship you have with Jesus? Is He opening a door for you because you are faithful, or do you find yourself banging up against walls and closed doors, and wondering why you are not progressing in your spiritual walk?

You may not feel like you have much strength, but Jesus promises that those who are faithful to His word, His church and His name will be given open doors to a richer, fuller, and more complete life. The door to a truly satisfying, purposeful, adventurous life begins when we walk in obedience to God. And those who walk through those open doors of opportunity are promised security, a home, a future, and an intimate relationship with the God of the universe. That is anything but boring!

If that's what you desire today, it begins by exploring and deepening your relationship with Jesus Christ. And that begins by talking to Him and reading His word.

Are you ready?

CHAPTER NINE

Laodicea: Sophisticated or Sanctified?

Have you ever been to a hot spring? I love them. I grew up 45 minutes away from Miette Hot Springs, a beautifully relaxing pool of sparkling warm water nestled in a crevasse of one of the Rocky Mountains.

The fun of going to Miette is two-fold. The first is the drive up there. Motorcyclists live for this road, RV drivers dread it -- 17 long, winding, twisting, turning, steep, precipitous kilometres of mountain road. In my dad's car, it was a great trip. Sure, a little slow, but beautiful nonetheless. When I drive my family up there, no one speaks. I'm not as ... cautious

... as my father. For the ride up, my wife gasps and pumps her imaginary brakes, the kids stare wide-eyed over the edge of the mountain, or watch out for the bears, deer, sheep, or whatever else is on the road. And I slip into a video-game coma, taking the steep Fiddle Valley corners with the same care and precision as I do when playing any number of my favourite driving simulators (Note: In the games I drive a two million dollar, 950 HP, Suzuki Esgundo Special Edition with a top speed of 200 Mph. In real life I drive a 180 HP, Dodge Grand Caravan).

However, if ... I mean when we get to the top, what greets us are the hottest mineral springs in the Rockies. When the water comes bubbling out of the mountain, it is usually at about 54°C, but then the water is cooled to a comfortable temperature of 40°C as it enters the pools. Next to the hot pools is the cold plunge where the water is only 7°C ... a decidedly refreshing temperature in contrast.

My family loves to drive up there near the end of the season, when the snow is beginning to fall, and sit in the hot pool, surrounded by the snow covered Rockies, watch the deer and mountain goats play, and let our worries melt away. Of course, in any other setting we'd look ridiculous in a toque and bathing suit, but there, it's standard attire.

This chapter talks an awful lot about hot and cold water, and about hot and cold believers.

But to start, and you definitely know by now what I'm going to say, grab your Bible again and read Revelation 3:14-22.

I'll wait here... No wait... Here. No, wait... HERE! No, no... definitely... here.

The Address

Done? As Paris Hilton would say, "That's hot" (You'll get that joke later). Laodicea was far and away one of the wealthiest cities of the ancient world, and was certainly the most affluent of the seven that we have studied so far.

They were located 40 miles from Philadelphia, on a several hundred-foot-high plateau which made the city near impregnable. It was at the junction of three important trade roads, and was known as one of the three "sister cities of the Lykos Valley," the others being Colosse (the same one that Paul writes to in Colossians), a few miles east, and Heiropolis, a few miles north. It was connected to the main road that led from Ephesus on the coast to the rest of Asia and the Orient. It was also on the route from the capital city of Pergamum to the Mediterranean coast. This was the megalopolis of the area.

This was a popular, well situated, wealthy city. It was well-known for its banks and financial institutions, sort of like the Toronto or New York of its day. It was also known for manufacturing rare black wool products that were made into everything from clothes to carpets and were exported throughout the Roman world. Not only that, but the temple to the Phrygian god Men Karou was also a medical school that invented a special eye salve out of alum that was used throughout the Mediterranean region to cure all sorts of eye problems.

Remember Watkins? Growing up there was always a little canister of Watkins' Petro-Carbo Salve in the bathroom in case we ever got hurt. I don't know what was in it, but anytime anything happened to anybody in the family, we'd pull out the Watkins and glop this miracle-goo all over the place. It was the cure-all at my house. That's what this alum eye salve was in its day. If there was an eye problem, mom would go to the cupboard and pull out the Men Karou Brand Eye Salve and slather it on.

Laodicea was also hit by the great earthquakes of 17 AD that we talked about during the study of the Philadelphia. While other cities were petitioning for money and aid from the Roman Emperor Tiberius so they could rebuild, Laodicea was the only one that had enough money to rebuild all by itself without imperial help.

One of the main *problems* with the city was that it had a poor water supply. The local water tasted absolutely putrid and nobody could drink it. So they built a six-mile-long aqueduct pipe coming from the south. Though the water was cool when it entered the pipe, by the time it reached the city, it had become lukewarm and was full of foul-tasting minerals. Not only did this large pipe make Laodicea easy to siege, because all you had to do was cut the pipe, but it also made the water in this city lousy to drink.

The church of Laodicea might have been planted by a man named Epaphras who is mentioned in Colossians 4:12-13, when Paul is sending along his final greetings at the end of the letter, and tells them to make sure that the letter he is writing to the Colossians makes it to Laodicea because they need to read it too.

John MacArthur calls this church "the last and the worst" of the seven churches in Revelation. In every other church there is a glimmer of hope, a nugget of optimism, a remnant of people who are faithful. Even in Ephesus, the church that had lost its first love, there were some that were still faithful. Even in Sardis, the dead church, there were a few that remained loyal and could be strengthened. But here in Laodicea, Jesus gives no good news, and mentions nothing positive. Laodicea is a lukewarm church that God is about to spit out of His mouth. The church disgusts him, just like the bad-tasting, rank smelling, tepid water of Laodicea.

Description of Jesus

Let's look at verse 14, "To the angel of the church in Laodicea write: These are the words of the Amen, the faithful and true witness, the ruler of God's creation." This church needed a reminder of who Jesus was, and so Jesus uses 3 divine titles for Himself.

First, He calls Himself "the Amen." *Amen* means, "so be it," or "may it be so"; something true and binding, firm, fixed and unchangeable. In Isaiah 65:16 we read, "Whoever invokes a blessing in the land will do so by the God of truth; he who takes an oath in the land will swear by the God of truth." The "God of Truth" is the God of "the Amen," and this passage in Isaiah tells us the importance of that word. When we say, "Amen," we are effectively invoking a "blessing in the land" in God's name. To us, God says, "Be careful with your 'Amens', they carry more weight than you think."

At the end of our prayers, or sprinkled around during our worship services, we often just tack on an "amen" to let everyone know we are done, because the song meant something to us, or because that's what we were taught to do. But when we say "Amen" at the end of our prayers, or during a sermon, or even during a worship song, what we are saying may be far more involved than we may think we're saying.

Amen is a *binding phrase* meaning that what we have just heard or spoken is the truth about God and His character, it's a statement to mean that we trust Him, and that any promises or commitments we've made, any scriptures read or covenants spoken will be *bound to us* as those who say "Amen"… "So be it"… "I agree." It is a *covenant word*, a word of promise, a word that affirms truth.

Jesus calls Himself "The Amen" because Jesus is the ultimate fulfillment of all of God's promises throughout the Bible. He was the fulfiller of all of the promises for salvation, judgment, mercy, grace, messiah, and restoration of the relationship lost in Eden. We trust God because we trust Jesus, know that He's never let us down or broken a promise, and know that He is the One who will follow through on all of God's promises. We believe all the promises we read throughout the rest of the book of Revelation, and throughout scripture, because we trust Jesus to never let us down.

Second, Jesus calls Himself "The faithful and true witness." This is a similar title to "the Amen." Jesus is simply saying that *what He says is true*. We can trust Him, what He says, and what He reveals through His word. He is *absolutely infallible* in His trustworthiness. He can claim this about Himself because there is no one that can bring accusation against Him and win their case. Only Jesus can claim to be "The Way, the Truth and The Life" and mean it.

One of the most frustrating things for the Pharisees and other people who were trying to destroy and discredit Jesus was that they couldn't find anything to bring against Him! They kept trying to find something wrong with Jesus, in His actions, His character, or His teachings, so they could finally pin Him down and destroy the confidence that people had in Him. They desperately wanted to find some proof of his fallibility, so they could accuse him, bring him before the authorities and publicly shame and disgrace Him. But no one could, so in the end they had to make it all up.

Jesus' third title for Himself is "the ruler of God's creation." The NIV is being generous here and is translating it so that we can understand better. Those who have a different translation have the words, "*the beginning* of God's creation." Some might read this and think that Jesus was the *first one created*, but the NIV helps us out when it uses the word "ruler."

The word "beginning," which is also an appropriate word here, is the Greek word ARCHE and means "origin" or "the person or thing that commences"... but not like a starting pistol, or a green light that begins a race ... it's more like the artist who "began" or was the "origin" of a painting; something that didn't exist and came completely out of the mind and effort of the artist. It was *through Jesus*, by Jesus, that all things were made. He was the one who "commenced" the process, and was the "origin" of all things. John 1:3 says, "Through Him all things were made; without Him nothing was made that has been made."

Jesus uses fiery words and strong titles that were meant to force the church of Laodicea, and all those who come after, to wrestle with what they believe about Jesus. Right from the first sentence, Jesus forces the people to ask themselves what they are doing, who they are worshipping, and who He is.

C.S. Lewis says that we have three choices about what we can do with the claims of Jesus. We can say He was either a *Liar*, a *Lunatic*, or the *Lord*.[vii] He was either *a Liar*, and claimed all these things for Himself, all the things recorded through the Gospels and the book of Revelation, *knowing* that He was lying ... which would make Him the most evil person ever. There have been literally millions of people that have followed after Him, finding His claims as their hope for their eternity, and suffering and dying by His word.

Or, He was a lunatic who really believed that He was God in the flesh, the Saviour of mankind, the Amen, the Faithful and true witness, and the ruler of God's creation ... but was actually nuts, and so would be anyone who follows Him.

Or, He *really* is who He says He is, and that means that we *really* have to decide what we are going to do with that information. If Jesus really is who He says He is, then we are required to make an enormous change in our lives. If He was a liar, we could dismiss it. If He was a lunatic, then we need to try to help all those who are following Him see that. But if He is the Lord, then our lives, and the way we perceive reality, is forever altered, and we *must* do something with that information, and it *must* change our lives.

The people of Laodicea were lukewarm in the way they looked at Jesus. Jesus uses these titles to let the church know that to be in relationship with Him is to be in relationship with the source of all creation, the ruler of the universe, the pre-eminent one in existence, the most powerful being in reality, and the most trustworthy and famous person ever. It is not something to be treated lightly, and not something to be set aside as a hobby or a trite distraction. He's not Santa Claus that comes once a year to bring presents, and not a 911 ambulance that we only need when we're in trouble. He's it. He's the one. And to be in relationship with Him is nothing short of mind-blowing.

The "I Know" Statement & The Diagnosis

Jesus diagnoses this church quickly and decisively. "I know your deeds, that you are neither cold nor hot. I wish you were either one or the other! So, because you are lukewarm—neither hot nor cold—I am about to spit you out of my mouth. You say, 'I am rich; I have acquired wealth and do not need a thing.' But you do not realize that you are wretched, pitiful, poor, blind and naked."

Laodicea's lukewarm water supply was a fitting metaphor for the worship and the activities of this church and the Christians within. Heiropolis to the north had beautiful, Miette-like hot springs, Colosse to the east had wonderfully cold water. By the time the water got to Laodicea it was lukewarm and tasted terrible. The local water supply was even worse because it was not only lukewarm and mineralized, but it stunk. It was like diving into or drinking swamp water. They were surrounded by stagnant water, filled with bitter and horrible tasting minerals--that's what this church's worship *tasted like* to God.

When we read these words of Jesus, sometimes we think that *hot is good* and *cold is bad.* That Jesus wants this church to be either hot on fire for him, or cold and dead. But that doesn't make sense; Jesus doesn't want any of His churches to be dead … so this probably isn't the best way to read it.

It's more likely that Jesus meant that He wished the church would be hot, like the thermal baths of Heiropolis where people would come to relax, to take away the stress of life, release their burdens, and find healing for their body and souls. Anybody who's been in a hot-tub knows this feeling. A place where you just soak your worries and troubles away.

The hot waters of Heiropolis would allow people to gather together, find peace, close their eyes and just be happy where they were outside the worries of the world. The hot water drew all sorts of people with maladies both physical and emotional, just like the hot springs today (which is also kind of gross when you're sitting next to the dude with the itchy-bumpy-red-flaky-skin problem who has come for the "healing effect"… true story). For whatever reason, many physical and emotional problems are temporarily relieved by sitting in hot water.

Of course, Jesus could also have meant "hot" as in the heat of a fire. Not a warm bath, but a fire that burns with intensity, consumes all that is around it, and motivates people to action. In Luke 24:32 we read about the reaction of two of the disciples who had been walking with Jesus after His resurrection as He was teaching them about the Bible, and the story of the Messiah found within. It says, "They asked each other, 'Were not our hearts burning within us while he talked with us on the road and opened the Scriptures to us?'" That's the kind of heat that Jesus wants.

And to be *cold* is not to be dead. Cold water is refreshing and pure. Think of an ice-cold bottle of water on a hot day, or plunging into a cold pool after doing yard work. It's refreshing, it wakes you up, makes you feel alive again. It is fun to be in and re-invigorates your body and soul. Jesus says, "I wish you were hot or I wish you were cold. But you're neither, you're lukewarm… and I can hardly stand you any more… you are both useless and disgusting… and I'm going to spit you out."

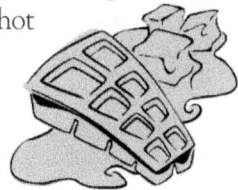

The church had become distasteful and unusable. The worship was repugnant to God. Their services weren't refreshing for those who came, nor was their church warm, relational, therapeutic or motivating to anyone. Anything they *were doing* was merely useless, selfish, busy-ness.

I want to park here for a second and take a look at two words that have been rolling around my head regarding lukewarmness. The words "sanctification" and "sophistication" (I was really helped in this by the book, "Every Man's Challenge" by Stephen Arterburn and Fred Stoeker, which I recommend that everyone read). *God wants us to be "sanctified"… the world wants us to be "sophisticated."* I think this is the root cause of the Laodicean problem, and my own lukewarmness; that we want to be sophisticated, not sanctified.

The word "sophisticated" has at its root the word "sophist," which is a very old word. A "sophist," which is from the Greek word SOPHISTES, means "to become wise or learned." The word SOPHIA means "wisdom." So a Sophist was a wise person. However, the word took a turn later and came to mean "one who gives intellectual instruction for pay," which isn't so bad … unless it is contrasted with the ancient Greek concept of the philosopher … meaning someone who taught for the love of teaching and passing on knowledge, and who would never take a cent for the honour of teaching his students. "Sophist" became a term of contempt. Ancient Sophists were famous for their clever, witty, just-inaccurate-enough arguments, like the slick lawyers or lobbyists of today. Smart sounding, but full of back-door trickery. The dictionary defines the word "sophisticated" saying it means, "To cause to become *less natural,* especially to make less naïve and *more worldly.* Or, to alter, pervert: to *sophisticate* beyond all recognition."

Laodicea, and many people today in and outside of the church, considers being "sophisticated" a good thing. But in truth, it's not a flattering word at all. Laodicea was a rich city, and the church considered itself to be a rich church. In Verse 17 Jesus says they say, "I am rich; I have acquired wealth and do not need a thing." There is no doubt that they claimed material wealth, but they were also claiming *spiritual wealth.* They equated their material wealth with blessing from God. Just look around their city, they were loaded with great stuff … just look around their church … they were rich! They figured that *God must really like what they're doing*! Jesus' teaching about "blessed are the poor, the meek, the hungry and the persecuted" didn't compute with this church.

With their wealth came an attitude of self-sufficiency. They didn't need anything. They were rich, *they were sophisticated.* They weren't like other people; they were "less natural, less naïve, and more worldly." They didn't need Rome's money to help them rebuild from the earthquakes, and they certainly didn't need Jesus to rebuild their lives. They were fine! They were sophisticated, but not sanctified.

The dictionary says the word "sanctify" means, "to make holy; set apart as sacred; to consecrate, to purify or free from sin." Their relationship with God was *meant* to set them apart from the world, not become more like it. All through the Bible we read God's command to "set apart for Him," "make holy," or "sanctify" various things.

The offering in the temples were to be *set apart* for Him, the Sabbath day was to be set apart for Him, some men in the army were to be set apart for a special mission, the tithe was to be set apart. Jesus is called the One who was "set apart as [God's] very own and sent into the world" (John 10:36). Paul and Barnabas were *"sanctified"* for God and sent out on missionary work. Peter tells us in 1 Peter 3:15 that we are to set apart, to sanctify in our hearts, Jesus Christ as our Lord. Elsewhere in 1 Peter 2:9,

Peter drives the point home when he says of Christians, "But you are a *chosen people*, a *royal priesthood*, a *holy nation*, a *people belonging to God*, that you may declare the praises of him who *called you out* of darkness into his wonderful light." He says over and over: you're different, you're different, you're different ... the church is not supposed to look like the world. It's different, it's sanctified.

I put together a little chart of what I'm talking about here. The differences between a sophisticated church and sanctified church; or a sophisticated person and a sanctified person.

Sophisticated Person	Sanctified Person
Change society first	Change themself first
Want to be seen & known	Want to see & know Jesus
Concern for church's reputation	Concern for Jesus' reputation
High-tech gadgets	High praise gatherings
New, cool programs	Old, old story
Outward appearances (clothes, skin)	Inward reality (character, joy)
Lobbying the government	Praying to God
Famous & popular preacher/pastor	Proclaim Jesus / Fame of God
Judge no one or everyone	Judge ourselves
They come to us	We go to them
Ashamed of "offensive scripture"	Knows the Gospel is offensive
Self-security	Security in Jesus
Self-esteem	Know depth of sin & grace
Quitters	Martyrs
Pop psychology	Biblical exegesis
Size	Depth
Outwardly impressive	Inwardly contrite
Nervous and busy	Content and exercised

John Stott said this: "The Laodicean church was a half-hearted church. Perhaps none of the seven letters is more appropriate to the 21st century church than this. It describes vividly the respectable, sentimental, nominal, skin-deep religiosity which is so widespread among us today. Our Christianity is flabby and anaemic. We appear to have taken a lukewarm bath of religion."[viii]

One of my pastor friends titled his sermon when he preached on Laodicea, "What makes God puke?" The answer? Lukewarm believers.

David Jeremiah said, "We are so afraid of being on fire for Christ; we don't want to be labelled as fanatics or extremists, yet in every other area of life we shed our proper manners and exude enthusiasm."[ix]

I completely understand this. I've yelled myself hoarse at hockey games. I couldn't talk the next day because I cheered so loud. I've walked out of movies moved to tears and scared to death. I've clapped my hands until they hurt at concerts just to hear an encore. I've told everyone I know about some of the products I've tried like razors, computer parts and musical equipment. Yet, I can't remember the last time, if ever, that I've left a church service hoarse from singing or worshipping.

I can count on one hand the amount of times I have been moved to tears, scared to death, sore from clapping, or stirred to the core as a result of a church service. And I know I've told more people about products I've tried than the Saviour I serve.

Ralph Waldo Emerson once said that "nothing great was ever achieved without enthusiasm." David Jeremiah adds, "…but much of our Christian experience is as limp as an overcooked noodle".[x] I think it's because I'd rather be sophisticated than sanctified. Many times I'd rather be seen well by the world than radically changed by God.

Jesus looks at this church and says in verse 17, "You say, 'I am rich; I have acquired wealth and do not need a thing.' But you do not realize that you are wretched, pitiful, poor, blind and naked." Jesus says that they may have looked sophisticated to the world, and even to themselves, but they didn't look like much to Him.

They were "wretched and pitiful." Not high and mighty, but disgusting and worthy of pity. They were "poor." They weren't rich in life, in joy, in peace or in anything that really matters on an eternal level. When it came to the stuff that matters, they were dirt poor. Jesus said in Matthew 16:26, "What good will it be for a man if he gains the whole world, yet forfeits his soul?" They were rich where it didn't matter and poor where it did.

They were also "blind" Jesus said. Their self-sufficient sophistication had led to a feeling that they didn't need anything … and that made them blind to what they really and truly needed. The path they thought was leading to success, security and happiness, was not one that led to heaven and Jesus, but one that led to hell.

They were also "naked," like the old story of the Emperor's New Clothes. Nakedness in the Bible refers to being spiritually defeated and humiliated. These people thought they were walking around in all their finery, but in truth they were spiritually naked. Not saved and forgiven, but defeated and humiliated.

The Prescription

So Jesus gives them their prescription in verse 18. He still loves these people and this church, and He really does want them to be healthy again. "I counsel you to buy from me gold refined in the fire, so you can become rich; and white clothes to wear, so you can cover your shameful nakedness; and salve to put on your eyes, so you can see." I want to explain these three.

First, "Gold refined in the fire, so you can become rich." There were lots of banks and money in Laodicea. Gold was the standard of wealth and earthly security, just like today, *but not if it was fool's gold* or

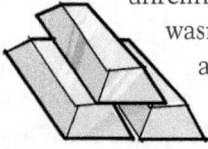

unrefined gold filled with other metals and dross; then it wasn't worth much. Jesus says if you really want a rich life, and have something of real value in your existence, then the world is not the place you want to buy from. He is the true source. Any other sources of currency will be tainted and fraudulent. They will seem worth something *at first*, but when truly examined, they will be seen to be worth very little; like a Fool's Gold Rush—everyone around is going crazy for this iron pyrite, but when it is examined by the expert, it's worth very little. Jesus says an ongoing relationship with Him, and His word, and His people, is the source of true treasure.

Here's a great thought: *What can we buy Jesus' gold with?* If this gold is of infinite purity and worth, and our possessions are worth nothing … and He's the only source … what does He expect us to buy it with?

With the only thing we have, the fool's gold that we are carrying around! If we are willing to part with the garbage that we think is so important and that we have been carrying around with us, that we have amassed and put so much credence in, and He wants us to turn it over to Him, then He will happily take it on trade for the real thing. That's mercy! But *we have to relinquish our old gold* to buy His new gold. We must surrender that which we *thought was valuable* before He will sell us that which *is truly precious.*

Second, He says to buy, "white clothes to wear." We covered most of this already. Laodicea was proud of their dying and cloth industry, especially of their black wool, which was famous all over the empire. The irony is this: although they were *neck-deep in fashions* and famous cloth, before God they were naked and ashamed.

Isaiah 61:10 says that one day the followers of God will be "clothed in righteousness." Some have taken this so far to say that when we get to heaven, we will be clothed for eternity in the good works we do on earth. What we have done in this world will be the clothing we wear in the next. Scary thought for some people! They might be walking around eternity almost in the buff! Jesus says that we need to come to Him to buy proper clothes to wear so that we can cover the shameful nakedness of a life lived without true righteousness.

Third, Jesus says to buy "salve to put on your eyes, so you can see." Laodicea's eye salve cured many eye problems, but not blindness – and certainly not spiritual blindness. Another irony is how the spiritually blind pride themselves on *having seen and experienced so many things in this world.* Have you had this conversation with someone? I have. I remember sitting and squirming my way through a conversation with a man that was recounting his "adventures" as a sailor. Some of the things that this man was laughing his way through were turning my stomach!

They've seen lots, been there, done that … they've run with that crowd, been to that club, drank that drink, done that drug, and performed that sexual conquest … but they are blind to the spiritual realities of what was going on around them! Jesus says that if they come to Him, and begin the relationship that finally opens their spiritual eyes to see what it's really like in this world, they will have a much different perspective on what they were *really doing*, where they *really were,* and *whose influence* they were under. And that kind of vision-healing only comes through Him.

True value in our lives is not in our fame, in our material possessions, our wealth or our perceived power. True value in our lives comes in a right relationship with God and each other, through Jesus Christ. Wherever you go after putting this book down, and wherever we are in the future, we will be constantly faced with the question of choosing *sanctification* or *sophistication.*

Our choice of the shows we watch on TV, the friends we associate with, the places we go to on Friday night, the movies we watch, books we read, church we attend, concerts we go to and leaders we trust will ask this question. Will they be great fashions of the world that look good to those around us but leave us naked before God, or will we choose a righteousness that *will* make us unpopular with the world but not ashamed to stand before God? Do we choose to live blind to reality, living in spiritual ignorance but *full of worldly knowledge*, or do we choose to be ignorant of sin and wide-eyed to God's glory?

In Verse 19 Jesus says, "Those whom I love I rebuke and discipline. So be earnest, and repent." To show us He cares for us, Jesus will never leave us the same. I don't want my kids to be the same as they are now forever. We must worry about the society that refuses to mature. I want my children to grow, mature, learn and become great adults. Jesus wants that for every one of us.

Jesus gives a second chance to this church. He's not being overly harsh here, but is giving everyone who has taken their relationship with Him for granted another chance to "be earnest" about their faith. He loves you and me and refuses to forget about us and our sanctification. Jesus implores us to "be earnest" about our connection with Him, meaning *really mean it, really work at it,* "and repent!" from not taking our relationship with Him seriously. Hot or cold!

If you Don't

Those who choose a future of lackadaisical, selfish religion, God will "spit out." That's it. God can only stand the hypocritical, play-acting, non-repentant, lukewarm, nominal Christians for so long. After that He's going to spit them out. Those who choose to be hot or cold will be saved and honoured. God will heat things up or cool things down to turn us into whom He wants us to be, at the temperature He wants us to be.

That's mercy! That's grace! That's God's love working itself out in our lives. He wants our lives to have purpose and fulfilment, and He'll do everything He can to give you the availability to let it happen.

If You Do

Jesus' promises to those who do obey are in verses 20-21. "Here I am! I stand at the door and knock. If anyone hears my voice and opens the door, I will come in and eat with him, and he with me. To him who overcomes, I will give the right to sit with me on my throne, just as I overcame and sat down with my Father on his throne."

These people felt satisfied, but they lacked a fundamental part of their existence: the presence of God in their lives. Was it possible that these people were so busy with their worldly distractions and pleasures that they would miss out on God Himself knocking on the door of their hearts? Would they opt for the pleasures of Earth over the pleasures of Heaven?

Money, sex, material possessions, sports and friends are all good things … unless they cause you to miss out on *God* knocking on the door of your heart -- and you end up living this life without Him! Anything that distracts from Jesus' call to salvation, repentance and fellowship with Him is a bad thing.

Notice that Jesus has so much respect for us that He's not just going to barge into our lives, but stands at the door and knocks. Some people need to accept Him for the first time, turning their lives over to Him, but some need to repent of their lukewarm faith and recommit their lives wholly to Him.

And Jesus says that He will "come in and eat with them." That phrase in the original language refers to the main meal of the day, supper: the big meal where friends and family and special guests are invited. It means that Jesus will not only come in and rearrange our hearts, and save our souls, but He will meet us as a friend and as a new member of His family.

He says next that he will "give the right to sit with me on my throne, just as I overcame and sat down with my Father on his throne." Jesus' victory over sin, death, hell, and Satan that was fought and won on the cross, will be passed along to all of those who are in His kingdom and who have a relationship with Him. Jesus reigns in heaven and on earth, and He will share that reign and power with each one in His family. They will be given a place of honour as conquerors and kingdom soldiers.

If the Shoe Fits

"He who has an ear, let him hear what the Spirit says to the churches." We started this whole thing by talking about thin ice. My parent's lake, not far from their house, had signs everywhere telling people to "stay off the ice" in the winter time. It doesn't stop people though, and someone goes through the ice every year. Despite the warning signs and the stories all over the area, people still walk, ride and even drive their vehicles onto the ice.

These seven letters are Jesus' personal letters and signs to those He loves, warning them about the thin ice they are walking on. They are His impassioned call out to them to wise up, get off the ice and back onto the solid ground of Biblical Christianity, and join Him where He is.

But these letters are not just for the church as a whole. They are also written as warnings and encouragements to everyone individually in the church, from then until today. When He says "I know," he is saying, "I know ... I've been there, and I'm with you right now." And He asks us to evaluate where we are, be convicted about our issues, and change our hearts. Which church has Jesus been using to tug at your heart?

The church in Ephesus may have looked good on the outside, but for all their busy-ness they lacked love. Their actions were not motivated by love for each other or for God, and so all of it was meaningless.

Smyrna was the persecuted church, full of people who were under vicious financial, physical and emotional attacks daily, and yet stood strong in their faith.

Pergamum was the church where we learned about Satan's side attacks. They stood firm at the front, but were being conquered by moral sin and compromise

Thyatira was the union church where Jezebel was; the church with the beautiful, politically correct, problem-solving teacher that was leading the church down the primrose path into heresy and sin. We learned how wise and discerning we need to be with our eyes and ears, and how important it was to know our Bibles and listen to God so that we don't compromise our faith and our relationship with Jesus.

Sardis was the dead church; the one that had the reputation for being alive but was really dead. It was the one that Jesus warned that they needed to "wake up!" and make their outside reputation match their inward reality.

We also looked at the church of Philadelphia. The small, ordinary, little church that only had a little strength left, that Jesus had nothing bad to say about. They had been obedient and faithful, despite the daily pressures to deny Jesus, and because of it Jesus opened a doorway of growth and opportunity in their life and church.

Each of these letters ends with a promise. A promise of what will happen to those "who overcome," those who are faithful until the end. I put them in a line to show what they sound like, and what Jesus says to those who are willing to live the sanctified life over the sophisticated one. He says He will:

1. Let them eat from the tree of eternal life in the paradise of God.
2. Give them the crown of life and protection from hell and punishment.
3. Let them eat the hidden manna, the spiritual food that truly satisfies.
4. Give them the white stone of acceptance and inclusion.
5. Give them a new name and a new destiny.
6. Give them authority over nations and victory in earthly battles.
7. Give them the Morning Star of hope in dark circumstances.
8. Clothe them in white, purity, forgiveness and victory.
9. Confess them as a victor and a citizen of Heaven before the Creator of the universe.
10. Have the doors of opportunity open before them.
11. Make their enemies look like fools.
12. Keep them secure through trials and tribulations.
13. Make them into the type of people who are secure, trustworthy, pillars of strength.
14. Give them a permanent home with Him.
15. Give them tattoos of the name of God, their new home and their new name.
16. Shower them with real, meaningful riches, open their eyes and have a personal relationship with them.

17. Give them the right to sit with Him on the throne of victory next to God the Father.

For those who believe in God, and believe that Jesus is His Son sent to earth to die for their sins, those who accept Him as Saviour and Lord, and serve Him uncompromisingly every day, Jesus lays out some immensely amazing, life-changing promises. And yet there are still millions of people in this world who *claim to know Jesus*, and yet it doesn't seem to show in their lives at all. They say they have faith in God, believe in Jesus, are filled with the Holy Spirit, and are part of the greatest organization in the world, but their lives are dull and lukewarm.

Jesus loves humanity dearly, so much so that He has sent these letters to call us back off the thin ice ... longing to pour out blessing and mercy in our lives ... but many of us seem to be content to keep walking out there, living in the doldrums of worldly boringness, masking their fake little lives with various distractions and entertainments ... instead of living tapped into the power and plan of Jesus Christ. We seek the temporary thrills of this world, the diversions of TV shows, sports, movies, sex, relationships, parties and whatever else ... which are not usually bad things ... but sometimes they cause us to miss out on the Big Reality and the greater blessing that Jesus wants to bring us as He asks us to give Him our whole hearts.

Somehow we are content to look at our families and think that the best we can expect is peace and quiet, and maybe some hugs and kisses, a hobby or two and sending our children off into the world to replicate that peace and quiet in their own families ... but we don't even realize the potential blessing that God wants for us if we'd be willing to fight the spiritual battle for our families, for purity in our own actions, for prayer in our lives, and the adventure of finding out what God wants for us if we'd be willing to walk His way. For some reason, for so many of us, our lukewarm life is good enough.

Is it good enough? Jesus asks us to make the choice. Sophistication or Sanctification. Jesus stands at the door and knocks. Will we answer, and will we live for Him?

Jesus' Letter to Me

I've always found it helpful when I've been able to put my thoughts down onto paper, particularly when studying a book. I don't know if you are "into journaling," or another exercise where you write your thoughts, prayers, scripture or study notes on a regular basis, but my hope is that this exercise begins or deepens that journey for you.

Let me encourage you to get your Bible again, a pen, and perhaps some extra sheets of paper, and work your way through this exercise. It's been a blessing for me to walk the steps of the Roman Road with you and read Jesus' letters together. God bless you on your journey.

Instructions:
1. Read Revelation chapters 1-3 in preparation for this exercise.
2. Spend some time in prayer:
    a. Read / Pray through Psalm 51.
    b. Confess any sins you may have and receive God's forgiveness.
    c. Ask God to help you answer the questions truthfully and meaningfully.

    d.   Commit this time to letting Him probe your heart and reveal His heart to you.
3. Fill in the blanks for Part 1.
4. Journal your responses in Part 2 (You may need a few more sheets of paper).
5. This exercise should take you more than an hour, depending on your time of prayer, reflection and depth of response.

Part 1

The Revelation Church I Identify With Most Is: _____

> Ephesus: Love in Priority
> Smyrna: Facing Persecution
> Pergamum: Flank Attacks
> Thyatira: Compromised Morality
> Sardis: Reputation and Reality
> Philadelphia: The Open Door
> Laodicea: Sophisticated or Sanctified

My Key Verse From This Letter Is (write the whole verse here):

_____

_____

_____

PART 2

1. The Address:

Who am I when no one is around?

Who would my friends, co-workers, and family say I am?

What are 3 of the most significant events of the past year, of the last five years, of my life (these can repeat if necessary)?

Past Year:

1.

2.

3.

Past 5 Years:

1.

2.

3.

My Whole Life:

1.

2.

3.

What patterns do I see in the story of my life?

2. Description of Jesus

Who is Jesus to me?

Who does the Bible say He is?

Which of the descriptions in Revelation 1-3 most impact me?

What name do I use when I pray (Father, Dear Jesus, Lord, God, Creator, Sir, Friend…)? Why?

3. "I Know"

If Jesus were to give me an evaluation of my walk with Him, He would say…

"I know your deeds…" What do I do in practice of my faith and relationship with Jesus?

"I know your afflictions…" What kind of struggles and suffering am I going through today?

"I know where you live…" What is special about the area of the city I live and at the place where I work? What spiritual / moral / relational temptations do I exist with day to day?

"I know your perseverance and maturity…" Am I persistent in my faith, or do I give up easily? How would I rate my spiritual maturity?

"I know your reputation…" Does my "reputation" match my "reality"?

"I know your open doors…" Is there an open door before me? Am I trying to walk through a closed door?

"I know your spiritual temperature…" Do I need cooling off (re-invigorating) or heating up (healing)? How worried about being "sophisticated" am I?

4. Diagnosis

Based on the reflections above, my main area(s) of strength is…

Based on the reflections above, my main area(s) of weakness is…

5. Prescription

The Lord Jesus is telling me I need to….

6. "If you don't..."

Of the judgments that Jesus says He will bring on the one who continues in sin, which most impacts / scares me? Why?

What will happen if I don't make these changes?

7. "If you do..."

Of the promises to the churches, which most impacts me? Why?

What do I want most out of my relationship with Jesus Christ?

What is He telling me during this exercise, and what do I believe He wants most for me?

8. If the Shoe Fits

When will I begin obeying and putting this into action?

What steps do I need to take?

Who will I ask to hold me accountable?

Do I need to talk to a deacon, elder or pastor about this?

Signature: _____ Date:_____

ENDNOTES

[i] The Preacher's Commentary Vol. 35, Earl F. Palmer, Pg 125

[ii] http://www.nationmaster.com/encyclopedia/Izmir,-Turkey

[iii] The Persecution of Christians Concerns Us All, Dr. Thomas Schirrmacher, Pg 49.

[iv] Escape the Coming Night, Dr. David Jeremiah Pg 66

[v] What Christ Thinks of the Church, John Stott, Pg. 72

[vi] http://wikipedia.org/wiki/Croesus

[vii] Mere Christianity, C.S. Lewis, Pg. 40-41

[viii] What Christ Thinks of the Church, John Stott, Pg 116

[ix] Escape the Coming Night, Dr. David Jeremiah, Pg 78

[x] ibid

www.ingramcontent.com/pod-product-compliance
Lightning Source LLC
LaVergne TN
LVHW021353080426
835508LV00020B/2269